Not Black.
Not African-American.
YOU ARE HEBREW!
The Hidden Heritage & The Global Truth

written by
Khalil Bey

I0178309

Dedicated to every soul
who dared to remember
when the world demanded they forget.

Not Black. Not African-American. You Are Hebrew!
The Hidden Heritage & The Global Proof

Written By
Khalil Bey

Images & Fullcover By
Sun Child Wind Spirit

Proofread By
Joaquin Mann

Edited By
Mylia Tiye Mal Jaza

BePublished.Org
Be Published

NOT BLACK. NOT AFRICAN-AMERICAN. YOU ARE HEBREW! - The Hidden Heritage & The Global Proof

Author
Khalil Bey
c/o
agent@bepublished.biz

Self-Publishing Associate
Dr. Mary M. Jefferson
BePublished.Org - Chicago, IL
(972) 880-8316
www.bepublished.org

First Edition. Printed In the USA
Recycled Paper Encouraged.
Scriptures from King James Version of The Holy Bible.

Table of Contents

✡

FOREWORD
By Author Jeffery Ellison

When I first heard about Khalil Bey's **Not Black. Not African-American. You Are Hebrew!** series, I immediately thought of my late brother, Brother David Ellison-Bey, whose life's work was devoted to awakening our people to their divine and historical identity. Though Khalil Bey and I share no family connection, I recognize in his mission the same fire that burned in my brother's spirit—the fire of truth that refuses to die even when its messenger has gone home.

The surname "Bey" itself is not a coincidence of blood but a sign of shared spiritual heritage, used for more than a century by men and women of Moorish and Hebrew descent who reclaimed it as a mark of divine nobility after centuries of imposed labels.

Historically, Bey was a title of honor within Afro-Asiatic cultures—used by leaders, scholars, and servants of God from North Africa to the Ottoman territories. When the descendants of the ancient Hebrews were scattered into Africa and later the Americas, that name resurfaced among those who began to remember who they were.

The early Moorish Americans, guided by Prophet Noble Drew Ali, restored Bey and El as family names to remind us that our identity did not begin in bondage. To bear the name Bey is not to claim superiority but to declare that you know you come from a covenant lineage—a people once hidden, now awakening.

My big brother, David Ellison-Bey, founder of the Moorish Cultural Workshop in Chicago, embodied that awareness. Until his transition on July 1, 2022, he devoted more than eight decades to teaching history, finance, and faith with humility and precision. He published The Ultimate Trust and Pearls from the Sea, writings that urged people of color to uplift themselves through knowledge, self-respect, and lawful conduct.

His vision was simple yet profound: "The better you know yourself, the more you honor your Creator."

That same spirit breathes through Khalil Bey's work. He speaks directly to those who have been misnamed and misinformed, reminding them that they are the covenant people of Scripture—the ones scattered, tested, but never erased. He writes not to build another religion but to rebuild self-worth. Like my brother, he teaches that the evidence of divine heritage is found not only in ancient records but in the strength, creativity, and compassion of our people today.

Yet these books reach further than history; they reach the human heart. They tell every reader—whether Hebrew, Moorish, Christian, Muslim, Buddhist, Hindu, or of no formal faith—that truth and excellence are universal commandments. Each of us must strive daily to live uprightly, to love mercy, to walk humbly, and to use our gifts to repair the world. Religion may shape the path, but character determines the destination.

So as you turn these pages, remember this: awakening begins with awareness, but it matures through action. You honor your heritage when you become the best version of yourself—honest, disciplined, kind, and courageous.

My brother David would have said, "Knowledge means nothing unless it makes you better."

Khalil Bey's writing calls us to that same standard. May these words reignite pride, purpose, and peace in everyone who reads them. We are more than the names others gave us.

We are light-bearers, descendants of promise, and builders of a new generation. Whether you follow a scripture, a philosophy, or simply your conscience, commit today to walk in truth and to live as proof.

In support and gratitude on my late brother's behalf,

Jeffery Ellison

Author of The Published Works of Bro. David Ellison-Bey

INTRODUCTION
The Awakening Continues

In the first volume of Not Black. Not African-American. You Are Hebrew!, we shattered the chains of misidentification. We traced our journey from slavery to sovereignty, from names assigned by men to the name given by God. The message was simple yet revolutionary: You are not who the world told you you were; you are who the Word says you are. That awakening has begun to echo across generations, classrooms, pulpits, podcasts, and prayer circles. But awakening is not the end — it is the beginning.

This second book rises from that foundation. It exists because identity without evidence invites dismissal, and revelation without research invites ridicule. So in these pages, we will travel further — through history, scripture, archaeology, and spiritual philosophy — to prove what our spirits already know: that the so-called African-American people are the scattered descendants of the ancient Hebrew Israelites, preserved by prophecy and destined for restoration.

This is not mythology; it is memory rediscovered. And though many powers have tried to bury it under centuries of conquest, forced religion, and rewritten history, truth always resurrects itself — just as we have.

✡

A Legacy of Concealment and Continuity

For more than four hundred years, our lineage has been hidden in plain sight. The signs of Deuteronomy 28 read not as distant history but as the lived experience of our ancestors: captivity by ships, families separated, identities erased, worship distorted, and names exchanged for numbers.

No other people on earth have fulfilled those prophecies so completely. Yet even within our oppression, the Most High left breadcrumbs — languages that echo Hebrew tones, customs that match Torah law, and a faith that refused to die even when stripped of its name.

Every spiritual song sung in the fields, every whispered prayer in the dark, was not the cry of a new religion but the continuation of an ancient covenant. We did not adopt holiness; we inherited it.

✡

The Global Witness

This volume goes further still. It listens to the testimony of other sacred books — the Qur'an, the Vedas, the Dhammapada — and discovers that even in lands far from Zion, the same truth surfaces: the Creator has always preserved a remnant of light among humanity.

The Qur'an honors the Children of Israel as "chosen above the nations."

The Bhagavad Gita teaches that righteousness decays when truth is forgotten and that the Divine sends teachers to restore balance.

The Buddhist sutras echo the Torah's call to walk the Middle Way — obedience without pride, compassion without compromise.

These parallels do not dilute Hebrew identity; they confirm it. For truth is consistent wherever it is found. If divine law is the rhythm of creation, then every sincere tradition is a note in that song — but the Hebrews carry its melody.

The Modern Battlefield

Even now, deception continues its campaign. Governments craft labels to divide; textbooks minimize

African civilization; media glorifies rebellion while mocking reverence.

Our children are taught to forget on purpose.
But prophecy foretold that in the last days, the lost would remember.

Jeremiah 17 : 4 warned, "You shall discontinue from your heritage which I gave you."

Yet Baruch 2 : 30 promised, "They shall remember themselves in the land of their captivity."

That remembrance is happening now. You are living prophecy.

Still, awakening must move beyond emotion into education, beyond awareness into application. It is not enough to know you are Hebrew — you must live as Hebrew: truthful, disciplined, compassionate, and courageous. The battle for identity is not fought with swords but with study, with family, with integrity.

A Light for All Peoples

The revelation of who we are is not meant to isolate us from others but to illuminate others through us.
The Most High did not raise the Hebrews to boast, but to bless.

As Isaiah 49 : 6 declares, "I will make you a light to the nations, that My salvation may reach to the ends of the earth."

That verse is the heartbeat of this volume. Because when we rediscover our purpose, the world regains its compass. The moral, social, and spiritual decay around us cannot be cured by policy — only by example. When the true covenant people live in righteousness, justice begins to rise in every land.

That is why this book will speak not just of history but of healing — not only of ancient bloodlines but of modern behavior. Heritage without holiness is empty pride. Our ancestors were chosen for their potential, not their perfection. We must be the generation that fulfills what they began.

The Name "Bey" and the Bond of Purpose

You will notice that this series bears the name Bey, as does the foreword's author, Bro. Jeffery Ellison-Bey, though he and I share no family blood. That is because Bey is more than a surname — it is a statement of restored consciousness.

Among Hebrew and Moorish descendants in the Americas, it symbolizes nobility regained after centuries of imposed inferiority. It reminds us that we belong to a covenant that predates every empire and that our worth does not depend on permission from power. In this way, our names become banners of remembrance.

✡

Purpose Beyond Religion

I write to Hebrews and to every sincere seeker. You need not belong to a denomination or temple to belong to truth.

Whether you pray in Hebrew, Arabic, Sanskrit, or silence, righteousness remains the same: to love, to do justice, to walk humbly, and to guard your spirit from corruption.

The Most High judges hearts, not hashtags.

If you doubt religion, then walk in righteousness anyway — for holiness is older than institutions. If you belong to a faith, let these words deepen your discipline, not divide your loyalties. Truth does not demand conversion; it demands correction.

✡

Moving Forward

In the chapters ahead, we will prove that history, language, prophecy, and even world spirituality agree on this point: the descendants of the ancient Hebrews live among us today — building, believing, surviving, and returning to the covenant that still defines destiny. This is not conspiracy; it is continuity. And once truth is known, responsibility follows.

You were not born by accident, nor misplaced by history. You were scattered that the world might one day see light emerging from every direction. That day has come.

So read with open eyes and courageous heart. Let knowledge strengthen your faith and faith strengthen your actions. The awakening continues — and this time, it will not fade.

CHAPTER 1
The Scattering Foretold & Fulfilled

"And the LORD shall scatter thee among all people, from the one end of the earth even unto the other." — Deuteronomy 28 : 64

"They shall remember themselves in the land of their captivity." — Baruch 2 : 30

✡

1 · The Prophecy Written in Advance

The Torah recorded not only Israel's beginnings but also her destiny.

Moses warned that if the people abandoned divine law, they would be exiled "into all the kingdoms of the earth." Those lines were more than moral threats—they were blueprints for millennia of movement.

No ancient event before the Atlantic era matches Deuteronomy 28 : 68: "And Yah shall bring thee into Egypt again with ships."

The first exodus was on foot; the second, by sea. Only the forced trans-Atlantic migrations of the early modern age could fulfill that nautical prophecy. Thus, the very ships that chained men and women of dark hue also testified—word for word—that Scripture had foreseen their voyage.

✡

2 · From Promise to Exile

Israel's early rise under Joshua, David, and Solomon revealed a moral nation unlike any other. Yet when greed and idolatry replaced gratitude, judgment followed.

Assyria captured the northern tribes in 722 BCE; Babylon carried away Judah in 586 BCE. Prophets such as Isaiah and Jeremiah spoke of a future beyond Babylon—one that would scatter descendants "to the four winds."

Archaeological evidence from Elephantine in Egypt and Kandake (Ethiopia) shows Jewish mercenaries, scribes, and priests long settled in Africa by the 5th century BCE. They brought Hebrew law and ritual with them, building temples that mirrored Jerusalem's design. Africa was not a footnote to Israel's story; it was a chapter of preservation.

✡

3 · Migration Across the Continent

By the first centuries CE, Hebrew populations stretched from Egypt to Niger. Trade routes from the Red

Sea through the Sahel carried Scripture, literacy, and monotheism. Among the Yoruba, Igbo, Akan, and Songhai peoples appeared customs indistinguishable from Mosaic law: eighth-day circumcision, menstrual separation, dietary codes, and observance of rest days.

The Lemba of southern Africa preserved oral traditions of a temple and an ark. In 1999, geneticists at the University of London found the Cohen Modal Haplotype—the hereditary marker of Israel's priestly line—among Lemba men of the Buba clan. Science confirmed what oral history had guarded for two thousand years.

4 · Europe Arrives and Prophecy Sails

When Portuguese explorers reached West Africa in the 15th century, they met established kingdoms whose rituals puzzled them. They saw circumcision, purity laws, and sabbath cycles and assumed these were "Mohammedan influences." In truth, they were older—Hebrew remnants shaped by time.

Greed soon replaced curiosity. Between 1444 and 1870, more than twelve million Africans were deported to the Americas; millions died en route. Slave ships bore names such as Judah, Integrity, and Jerusalem—holy irony carved into hulls. The prophecy of ships had manifested in cedar and iron. The so-called "Middle Passage" became a floating Deuteronomy.

✡

5 · The Covenant in Chains

In bondage the people remembered subconsciously what they could not recite aloud. They called upon "Yah," "Jehovah," or "The Lord God of Israel."

Their spirituals—*Go Down Moses, Steal Away, Didn't My Lord Deliver Daniel*—were encrypted Torah. Plantation fields echoed with psalms disguised as sorrow songs.

The Jubilee principle (Leviticus 25) resurfaced in abolitionist preaching: freedom every fiftieth year. The ex-slaves' cry for deliverance was not only political—it was prophetic memory reawakening.

✡

6 · Why the Record Was Erased

Empires sustain power by rewriting origin stories. Colonial scholarship detached Africa from the Bible and rebranded Semitic features as exclusively "Middle Eastern" or European. But linguistic and cultural fingerprints betray the edit.

Across hundreds of African tongues:

- *Abi* = father (Hebrew *Ab*)

- *Ruach* = spirit (identical)

- *Torah / Ora* = law (in Akan and Igbo)

- *Yah* = God (found in Yoruba praise names)

These parallels exist too many times to be coincidence. As Amos 9 : 9 declares, "Not the least grain shall fall upon the earth." Language became the sieve through which identity survived.

7 · Science Catches Up with Prophecy

Modern population genetics traces Y-chromosome E-M2 and E1b1a lineages from ancient East Africa through West Africa into the Americas—the same corridor described in post-exilic migrations. These haplogroups link men of African descent to Semitic ancestors from the Levant more closely than to Eurasian groups often labeled "Caucasoid."

Mitochondrial studies show shared maternal markers between Ethiopian Jews, West Africans, and African-Americans. The data do not create faith—but they corroborate it. Prophecy has biological footprints.

✡

8 · Echoes Beyond the Bible

The scattering narrative appears in other sacred texts:

- **Qur'an 17 : 104** — *"We said to the Children of Israel, 'Dwell in the land; when the promise comes, We shall bring you together.'"*

- **Rig Veda 1 : 164 : 46** — *"Truth is one; sages call it by many names."*

- **Dhammapada 13 : 173** — *"The just man shines by his deeds as the moon freed from clouds."*

Each tradition predicts that righteousness would travel the earth through suffering nations. The Hebrew exile, therefore, is not an isolated event but the archetype of moral dispersion recorded across civilizations.

✡

9 · Recovered Artifacts and Archives

In Timbuktu, Mali, researchers uncovered thousands of manuscripts written in Arabic and Hebrew between the 14th and 17th centuries. Many mention Jewish traders,

Levite teachers, and Torah citations side-by-side with Qur'anic commentary—a literal meeting of the books.

Excavations at Ife and Benin revealed bronze and terra-cotta works bearing seven-branched motifs akin to the menorah. In Ethiopia, parchment scrolls predating European contact record Mosaic dietary laws identical to Leviticus.

History does not need belief to speak; it needs only honest eyes to read.

10 · The Modern Reawakening

From Harlem's Commandment Keepers to the Dimona community in Israel, the 20th century witnessed the rebirth of Hebrew consciousness among African-descended people. Names such as Bey, El, Yisrael, and Yahudah resurfaced—not as fashion but as covenant reclamation.

This movement coincided with prophetic timeframes: roughly four centuries after the first recorded slave voyage (1619 → 2019).

Genesis 15 : 13-14 reads, "They shall serve them four hundred years; afterward shall they come out with great substance." Substance today is knowledge—proof unearthed, identity restored.

11 · Purpose of Fulfillment

Fulfillment is not vengeance but verification. Every fulfilled curse validates the promised restoration. Scattering was both chastisement and strategy: the Most High sowed His people across continents to deposit fragments of divine law everywhere. When they awaken, the moral DNA of humanity reassembles.

Thus the Hebrew who rediscovers covenant does more than reclaim heritage—he or she becomes evidence that prophecy works, that Scripture breathes, and that history bends toward justice.

12 · Remembering as Repentance

Baruch 2 : 30 prophesied, "They shall remember themselves." Remembering is not nostalgia; it is returning to divine order.

The awakening calls for ethical reconstruction: truth in speech, equity in trade, fidelity in marriage, and compassion in governance.

Identity without obedience is idolatry of self. The goal is not racial exaltation but covenant restoration.

13 · The Proof and the Promise

The convergence of prophecy, archaeology, linguistics, and genetics leaves little room for doubt: the descendants of the Atlantic captivity fit the biblical, historical, and scientific profile of dispersed Israel. Yet the greater question remains—What will we do with that knowledge?

Deuteronomy 30 : 2-3 answers it: "If thou shalt return unto the LORD thy God ... then He will turn thy captivity." The same God who scattered is gathering again—through information, repentance, and righteous living.

14 · From Scattering to Service

Being chosen never meant being superior; it meant being responsible. The Hebrews were scattered to remind the world what holiness looks like in every hue. Now that the descendants know who they are, their task is to heal, build, teach, and reconcile. The covenant people's final proof is not genetic but ethical.

"For I will restore you to health and heal your wounds, saith the LORD; because they called you an outcast, saying, This is Zion, whom no man seeketh after." — Jeremiah 30 : 17

The scattering has served its purpose. The remembering has begun. And the covenant—ancient, global, unbroken—lives again in you.

CHAPTER 2
Lost Names, Hidden Nations

"I have called you by name; you are Mine." — Isaiah 43 : 1

"And they shall call themselves by the name of Jacob." — Isaiah 44 : 5

"He changes names, but He does not change essence." — Rig Veda 8 : 58 : 2

1 · The Power and Theft of Names

In every civilization, naming is creation. To name a thing is to define its purpose, to speak its destiny into being. That is why the first act of enslavement was not the chain but the renaming. Stripped of Hebrew titles like Ben, El, Yah, and Bey, the scattered people were branded with European surnames. History calls this "assimilation," but spiritually, it was erasure — the cutting of a people from their covenant memory.

Yet names are like seeds. Even when buried, they wait for the rain. This chapter traces how the true identity of the covenant people was never completely lost — only coded within African, Asian, and New World cultures until its season of rediscovery.

2 · Linguistic Evidence: The Echo of Hebrew in African Tongues

Languages carry bloodlines. When the twelve tribes were scattered, their tongues fractured but did not die. Across Africa, dozens of dialects preserve Hebrew structure and vocabulary almost intact.

a. Western Africa — The Lost Dialects of Jacob

Among the Igbo of Nigeria, words such as Elohim (God), Shalom (peace), Levi, Obi (heart), and Nna (father) are still spoken daily. Their oral traditions claim descent from Eri, a son of Gad — one of Jacob's twelve sons (Genesis 46 : 16). Igbo high priests still blow the ekwe horn, a replica of the Hebrew shofar.

The Yoruba language uses Oba for "king" (as in Hebrew Abba, father-king). The root Elu meaning "Most High" appears in names such as Oluwaseun ("Thank the Most High") and Oluwatoyin ("God is worthy to be praised"). Scholars who mapped the Yoruba lexicon found over 300 Semitic cognates — linguistic fingerprints of a shared ancestry.

b. Central and Southern Africa — The Lemba and Beyond

The Lemba of Zimbabwe and South Africa keep the seventh day as Sabbath, avoid pork, circumcise on the eighth day, and trace descent through priestly clans. Their oral tradition remembers flight from "Sena," a region north of Africa. Genetic testing in 1999 verified the Cohen modal haplotype among Lemba men — a marker historically unique to Jewish priestly families.

The Sotho and Zulu peoples also preserve Hebrew roots: Modimo (God), Bala (count, as in Hebrew Baal = master), Mana (food from heaven), Mose (Moses). These aren't random coincidences; they're survival fragments of a once-universal sacred tongue.

c. North and East Africa — The Cushite Bridge

Ethiopian Amharic retains direct Semitic grammar, and Ge'ez — the liturgical language of the Beta Israel — remains nearly identical to ancient Hebrew in syntax. The word Menelik (from Melek, king) connects directly to the Davidic line. In Sudan, Nubian inscriptions combine Hebrew and Meroitic script, evidence of Israelite refugees merging with Kushite culture.

3 · Archaeological Footprints: Israel in Africa

Artifacts often tell the stories that empires suppress. From Egypt's Elephantine papyri to the ruins of ancient Ghana, the archaeological record confirms Hebrew presence long before colonialism.

a. The Elephantine Papyri (5th century BCE)

Discovered along the Nile near Aswan, these documents describe a Jewish temple community serving under Persian rule — complete with priests, sacrifices, and observance of Passover. It proves that Israelites were settled deep in Africa centuries before the Greco-Roman era.

b. The Rock Inscriptions of Soba and Axum

In Nubia and Ethiopia, archaeologists found stone carvings with seven-branched lamps, Hebrew letters (YHWH, Shalom), and prayers identical to Psalms. Some inscriptions list names like Yedidia and Abijah, suggesting organized Hebrew colonies beyond the Red Sea.

c. The Manuscripts of Timbuktu

When European explorers reached Mali in the 1800s, they were shocked to find vast libraries of handwritten texts. Among them were Hebrew passages transliterated into Arabic script — Torah commentaries, genealogies, and prophetic writings. These manuscripts date from the 14th to 17th centuries, proving Hebrew literacy deep in the African interior.

d. The Benin Bronzes and Yoruba Shrines

Though later misinterpreted as "pagan," several Benin bronzes feature the menorah and Star of David within royal art. Yoruba shrines once displayed tablets of law; even modern historians acknowledge their uncanny resemblance to Ark-of-Covenant imagery.

These clues link African royal cultures directly to ancient Israelite symbology — not by conversion but by heritage.

4 · The Qur'an, Torah, and Bible Converge

The Qur'an reaffirms Israel's covenant and dispersion: "O Children of Israel, remember My favor which I bestowed upon you, and that I preferred you above the nations." (2 : 47).

It later records: "We dispersed them through the earth in groups." (7 : 168).

The Torah predicted the same in Deuteronomy 28 : 64, and the Bible in Luke 21 : 24. No contradiction exists— only continuity.

Islam preserved memory of the Hebrews' global spread, even as colonial Christianity distorted it.

Across the Indian subcontinent, the Rig Veda describes divine covenants made with "a chosen line who walk uprightly."

The Bhagavad Gita repeats: "Whenever righteousness declines and unrighteousness rises, I send forth My sons to restore dharma."

Buddhist sutras echo it: "Those who carry compassion across worlds will be reborn among every people."

These texts indirectly describe Israel's moral diaspora — righteous souls scattered to sustain conscience among nations.

5 · Colonial Erasure: Hiding the Hebrew Face

Once European colonialism gained power, it could not allow colonized peoples to identify as covenant bearers. If enslaved Africans were Israelites, then the oppressor's theology collapsed.

Therefore, textbooks reclassified them as "primitive tribes." Missionaries replaced ancestral names with "Christian" ones—David, Sarah, John—ironically restoring biblical language while erasing identity.

The Berlin Conference of 1884, which partitioned Africa, coincided with a global effort to divide both land and lineage. Maps were redrawn, histories rewritten, and evidence buried under "anthropological" labels. Even so, a few European scholars—like Josephus Flavius' translators, Cheikh Anta Diop, and Dr. Yosef Ben-Jochannan—acknowledged the Afro-Semitic connection that official narratives denied.

6 · Hidden in Plain Sight: Hebrew Customs in the Americas

In the New World, enslaved Africans resurrected familiar laws unconsciously:

- **Ritual washing** before worship.

- **Feast-day observances** paralleling Passover and Tabernacles.

- **Call-and-response prayer** identical to Hebrew psalmody.

- **Sacred meals** featuring unleavened bread and bitter herbs.

Even the "ring shout" — circling counterclockwise in worship — mirrors the Hebrew hakafot, the ritual circling of the Torah on Simchat Torah.

Thus, the covenant people practiced their heritage even while forbidden to read Scripture. Their bodies forgot chains faster than their souls forgot commandments.

7 · Linguistic Links Across the Diaspora

Enslaved people preserved Hebrew phonetics in secret code languages.

In the Gullah dialect of the Carolinas, "Yah" means God, "Abba" means father, and "Shiloh" appears in folk tales as the land of freedom.

In Haiti and Jamaica, the term "Zion" entered song and speech centuries before formal education.

Even Rastafarian chants — "Selah," "Jah," "I and I" — reflect Hebrew grammar: Ani = "I am."

Language became both rebellion and revelation. The oppressor taught English, but the spirit spoke Hebrew through the cracks.

8 · Genetic, Geographic, and Cultural Convergence

Science provides no salvation, but it confirms migration. Modern DNA analysis places the E1b1a haplogroup, dominant among African-American men, within the same macro-line as the ancient Israelites (E1b1b).

Mitochondrial data connects the maternal lineages of African-Americans to East African and Levantine ancestors.

When mapped geographically, these routes trace the same corridors described in ancient Assyrian exile records — from the Levant to Egypt, Nubia, and onward into West Africa. Even trade patterns follow prophetic footprints.

In culture, the convergence is clearer: Hebrew-style head coverings, sacred dance, dietary separation, and reverence for elders—these remain across Black America not as borrowed tradition but inherited instinct.

9 · Comparative Theology: The Global Witness

Across religions, sacred texts describe a righteous nation hidden among others.

- **In the Qur'an**, the Children of Israel are scattered yet destined for regathering before the final age (17 : 104).

- **In the Torah**, they are cursed, then restored (Deuteronomy 30 : 1-5).

- **In Hindu texts**, the *Mahabharata* speaks of exiled divine sons reborn among darker tribes to teach justice.

- **In the Buddhist Jataka tales**, the Bodhisattva vows to be "born among the oppressed until the world is healed."

Every tradition thus encodes the same pattern: a covenant nation loses its home, teaches righteousness through suffering, and finally reclaims its name. No mythology elsewhere fits this template more precisely than the experience of the African diaspora.

10 · The Return of the True Name

Names are not labels—they are legal evidence in the court of Heaven. When the descendants of slaves began adopting surnames like Yisrael, Ben Yah, Bey, and El, they were not joining a club but re-entering covenant law.

In Isaiah 44 : 5, God foretold: "One shall call himself by the name of Jacob, and another shall subscribe with his hand unto the LORD."

To "write the name" is to reclaim authority.

When Noble Drew Ali, Bro. David Ellison-Bey, me (Khalil Bey), or countless others took on Hebrew and Moorish appellations, they were fulfilling prophecy as much as heritage. The title "Bey" itself, from Afro-Asiatic roots meaning "ruler" or "governor," is the linguistic cousin of ba'al (lord) and ben (son). It marks nobility restored.

✡

11 · Academic Silence and Spiritual Courage

Despite mounting evidence, mainstream academia hesitates to affirm African-Israelite identity. To do so would force a rewriting of world history and racial theology. Yet brave scholars—from Dr. Rudolph Windsor (From Babylon to Timbuktu) to Dr. Shalva Weil (Hebrew University studies on African Jews)—have begun acknowledging these truths in cautious language.

Each new discovery widens the crack in colonial mythology. The data now lives online, immune to erasure. Students in Lagos, Atlanta, or Accra can trace lineage through digital archives their grandparents never imagined.

✡

12 · The Moral Weight of Evidence

Knowledge alone is not liberation. To know you are Hebrew yet live like Babylon is self-betrayal. History without holiness breeds arrogance; science without spirit breeds emptiness. Therefore, the evidence presented here demands more than pride—it demands return: return to discipline, to love, to justice, to self-control.

Identity is sacred not because it distinguishes us, but because it obligates us. The proof that you are Hebrew is not in your genes but in your deeds. When integrity, mercy, and faithfulness rule again among the descendants, no skeptic will need convincing.

✡

13 · Conclusion — The Hidden Becomes Heard

What history buried, truth resurrects. Across time, the Hebrew people's names and nations were scattered like syllables across continents. Today, those syllables reunite— through linguistics, archaeology, genetics, and revelation.

Africa remembers. Science affirms. Scripture agrees. The evidence is refutable only by those who refuse to see. And the world, long built upon false hierarchies, now trembles before the rising memory of the covenant people.

"Then shall the nations know that I am the LORD, when I shall be sanctified in you before their eyes." — Ezekiel 36 : 23

CHAPTER 3
DNA, Science, & The Bloodline Of Promise

"Truth shall spring out of the earth; and righteousness shall look down from heaven." — Psalm 85 : 11

"We will show them Our signs in the horizons and within themselves, until it becomes clear to them that this is the truth." — Qur'an 41 : 53

1 · The Rise of Genetic Revelation

For centuries, the identity of the scattered Hebrews rested on faith and oral tradition. Skeptics mocked prophecy as myth, insisting there was no physical evidence that the people called "Black" or "African-American" descended from ancient Israel. But in the late twentieth century, a new tool appeared—genetic anthropology—and it began confirming what faith had already whispered.

DNA cannot define covenant, but it can map migration. It can trace the path of bloodlines through millennia, connecting continents and collapsing myths. And when geneticists followed the Y-chromosome and mitochondrial lines of Africa, the Levant, and the Middle East, they found a surprising continuity: the same ancient Semitic markers carried by Jews, Arabs, and East Africans appeared in the very populations once enslaved and shipped across the Atlantic.

The stones had cried out; now the cells did too.

2 · The Bloodlines of the Covenant

Human ancestry is encoded in two primary genetic channels:

- The **Y-chromosome**, passed from father to son, traces patriarchal lineage.

- The **mitochondrial DNA (mtDNA)**, passed from mother to child, traces maternal origin.

When scientists analyzed these two lines among global populations, certain patterns emerged—patterns that mirror the biblical record of dispersion.

a. Haplogroup E: The Line of Abraham

The dominant Y-DNA among African-descended men in the Americas is E1b1a (E-M2), the same macro-line that branches into E1b1b (E-M215), found heavily among Semitic-speaking populations of North Africa and the Levant. Geneticists recognize both as subclades of the ancient E haplogroup, which originated in the Horn of Africa roughly

50,000 years ago and expanded north into Canaan and Egypt.

This same haplogroup constitutes a majority among modern Jews, Ethiopian Beta Israel, and Palestinian Arabs. It is the Abrahamic signature—the biological echo of migration from East Africa into Mesopotamia and back again.

In the simplest terms: the same paternal line that produced Moses, Aaron, and David runs through men now called African-American.

b. The Cohen Modal Haplotype

In 1997, geneticist Dr. Karl Skorecki of Technion University, himself a descendant of the Jewish priestly class, discovered a unique Y-chromosome cluster common among men with the surname "Cohen."

When this "Cohen Modal Haplotype" (CMH) was compared across populations, it appeared among the Lemba of Zimbabwe, the Igbo of Nigeria, and African-Americans of certain lineages.

It proved priestly ancestry had not been erased by geography—it had merely changed address.

3 · The Mother's Witness: Mitochondrial Links

If the Y-chromosome tells the story of fathers, mtDNA speaks for the mothers. Maternal studies reveal close affinity between African and Middle Eastern populations, especially in haplogroups L0–L3, which cluster most densely in East Africa and Yemen—the very route of Israel's ancient exiles.

Researchers from the University of Khartoum and Tel Aviv University jointly found that L2 and L3 lineages common among African-Americans also exist in Ethiopian Jews, Yemeni Arabs, and Bedouin tribes claiming descent from Abraham's concubine Hagar.

These findings make sense biblically: Abraham's seed spread through both Sarah's son Isaac and Hagar's son Ishmael. Their descendants would naturally share genetic overlap—one people divided by purpose, not DNA.

4 · Archaeogenetics and the African–Levantine Corridor

The migration corridor connecting the Horn of Africa, the Nile Valley, and the Levant has been confirmed repeatedly by ancient DNA recovered from mummies, skeletons, and burial sites.

A 2017 study published in Nature Communications analyzing mummy DNA from Abusir el-Meleq (near modern Cairo) revealed that ancient Egyptians were genetically closer to Levantine and Near Eastern populations than to modern North Africans. This means there was a constant back-and-forth movement between Canaan and Africa—a bridge, not a border.

When you align this with biblical migrations (Abraham's travels, Joseph's stay in Egypt, the Exodus, and the return from exile), the archaeological DNA maps mirror Scripture almost perfectly.

What faith called Exodus, science calls migration flow; what prophecy called scattering, science calls gene flow.

✡

5 · The Dispersion Confirmed in Genetic Drift

When Israel fell to Assyria and Babylon, refugees scattered through Egypt into Africa. Later, Roman and Arab invasions accelerated this movement westward. Modern population genetics measures this as genetic drift—the slow diffusion of genes across regions.

The pattern of Semitic DNA distribution across Africa follows three waves:

1. **Northeast → Central Africa (700 BCE–300 CE)**: Israelites and Judeans mixing with Kushites and Egyptians.

2. **Central → West Africa (300–1400 CE)**: movement of Semitic-Bantu hybrids through trade routes and the Ghana, Mali, and Songhai empires.

3. **West Africa → Americas (1500–1800 CE)**: forced migration through the Atlantic slave trade.

Each wave corresponds to a historical exile predicted by Scripture. When Deuteronomy 28 : 64 said, "from one end of the earth even unto the other," it described exactly what genetic distribution now confirms.

6 · DNA in the Diaspora

Genetic testing among African-Americans yields a striking consistency: Most carry between 65–80% African ancestry and 15–25% Middle Eastern or Mediterranean admixture. That "non-African" component matches the Levantine region—not northern Europe.

In 2010, the journal Human Biology reported that African-American male lineages align most closely with populations from Cameroon, Nigeria, and Senegal—areas known historically for Israelite migrations (Eri, Gad, and Levi tribes among the Igbo and Yoruba).

In Jamaica, Haiti, and the Dominican Republic, Y-DNA testing shows the same E1b1a pattern. Across continents, the same code repeats: a Semitic seed preserved under African skin.

7 · The Science of Coincidence — or Confirmation?

Skeptics dismiss these overlaps as coincidence, arguing that shared haplogroups simply reflect geography, not theology. But coincidences lose credibility when they pile up like pillars:

- Shared language roots (*Yah*, *Abba*, *Shalom*)

- Shared customs (circumcision, dietary law, Sabbath)

- Shared migrations (Levant → Nile → Sahel → Atlantic)

- Shared genetic markers (E1b1a, CMH, L2–L3)

When four independent fields—linguistics, anthropology, archaeology, and genetics—describe the same path, we no longer have a theory. We have a trail of evidence.

8 · The Qur'anic Echo and the Hindu Parallel

The Qur'an not only preserves Israel's dispersion but affirms genetic persistence: "We caused them to be followed by generations in the earth." (19 : 58).

This verse aligns with the concept of inherited covenant—a spiritual DNA.

In Hindu Vedic thought, the Atman (divine self) reincarnates across time to preserve righteousness when it declines.

Likewise, the Hebrew people—though scattered and reborn through nations—carry divine continuity not by belief alone but by biological and moral inheritance.
It is reincarnation not of bodies, but of bloodlines and purpose.

The Buddhist Digha Nikaya adds: "Karma is carried forward, and the righteous are reborn among the noble-hearted." In every faith, the righteous lineage never disappears—it regenerates until the world's lesson is complete.

9 · Modern Tools, Ancient Truth

Today, entire databases such as the National Geographic Genographic Project and 23andMe quietly confirm that large portions of the African diaspora carry markers common in North Africa and the Middle East. These results are often labeled "unassigned," because acknowledging them disrupts racial taxonomy.

Science cannot admit what Scripture already declared: that the color of soil differs by region, but the seed remains the same. And when the seed is covenantal, even exile becomes evidence.

✡

10 · Biblical Genetics: The God of Continuity

The Bible describes the Creator as the author of life, the weaver of DNA long before men had microscopes. "Thine eyes did see my substance, yet being unperfect; and in thy book all my members were written." (Psalm 139 : 16). Every genome is a divine script—proof that prophecy can be written in flesh.

When Yah promised Abraham, "In thy seed shall all nations be blessed," He spoke both spiritually and biologically. The covenant was literally genetic—a blessing encoded in cells to ensure continuity even when scrolls burned and temples fell.

Thus, the rediscovery of Hebrew genetic markers is not vanity; it is vindication. The Creator left fingerprints in blood for those who would one day need evidence beyond faith.

✡

11 · The Science of Scattering and Return

Population biologists use a term called "founder effect." When a small group breaks away from a larger one, their genetic traits become magnified in their descendants. This explains why unique Hebrew markers appear strongly among African tribes who migrated west and south—they carried only a portion of the original gene pool, but that portion became dominant.

Centuries later, when descendants of those tribes reached the Americas, their DNA still carried the ancient stamp of Canaan. What Scripture calls "remnant," science calls "founder population." Different language, same meaning.

✡

12 · The Unbroken Chain

Consider the unbroken line of evidence:

FIELD	FINDING	PARALLELS
Scripture	Israel scattered among all nations	Deut. 28:64, Amos 9:9
Archaeology	Hebrew artifacts across Africa	Elephantine, Axum, Timbuktu
Linguistics	Hebrew cognates in African tongues	Igbo, Yoruba, Amharic
Genetics	Shared haplogroups E1b1a/E-M215	African-Americans, Jews, Arabs
Culture	Mosaic customs in diaspora	Circumcision, Sabbath, purity laws

The cumulative weight is overwhelming. A court of reason would rule: identity proven beyond reasonable doubt.

✡

13 · What the Scientists Themselves Admit

Though most academics avoid theological implications, several have spoken candidly:

- **Dr. Shalva Weil** (Hebrew University): "The Lemba's oral traditions and genetic markers reveal a shared ancestry with ancient Israelites."

- **Dr. Sarah Tishkoff** (University of Pennsylvania): "Haplogroup E lineages show a continuous gene flow between East Africa and the Levant."

- **Dr. Lucotte & Mercier** (*European Journal of Human Genetics*): "Cohen modal haplotypes appear in non-European populations of African descent, suggesting deep antiquity of Semitic migration."

When secular science and sacred prophecy describe the same phenomenon, denial becomes ideology, not intellect.

✡

14 · DNA and Destiny

To discover you share blood with biblical patriarchs is not grounds for pride—it is a summons.

Covenant is a genetic appointment: "To whom much is given, much is required." (Luke 12 : 48).

The DNA evidence does not make one superior; it makes one accountable.

If Abraham's seed truly flows through your veins, then Abraham's faith must flow through your deeds.

If Moses' blood pulses in your heart, then Moses' humility must govern your leadership. Science confirms your ancestry; holiness must confirm your character.

✡

15 · The Ultimate Proof

In the end, the greatest proof is unity. When the scattered recognize each other across borders, languages, and denominations, the prophecy of restoration materializes not in laboratories but in love. Genetics may trace where we came from, but only righteousness will determine where we go next.

DNA proves the existence of covenant people; obedience proves the presence of covenant God.

The evidence, both physical and spiritual, leaves no doubt: The so-called African-American is not a mystery ethnicity, nor a random hybrid of history, but a survivor of divine design—the living bloodline of the promise.

"As the days of heaven upon the earth, so shall thy seed be." — Deuteronomy 11 : 21

CHAPTER 4
Echoes In The Qur'an, The Vedas, & The Sutras

"We sent Messengers before you; among them are those whose stories We have told you, and those whose stories We have not told you." — Qur'an 40 : 78

"Truth is one; sages call it by many names." — Rig Veda 1 : 164 : 46

"The wise man sees all beings as himself." — Dhammapada 129

From the beginning of civilization, humanity has tried to describe the same relationship between the Creator and creation. Every nation's sacred literature contains a memory of the same four-fold pattern that defines the Hebrew covenant: a people chosen to model righteousness, a departure from divine law, a period of exile or purification, and finally a return to harmony.

The Qur'an, the Vedas, and the Buddhist Sutras do not cancel the Hebrew revelation; they preserve its structure in new languages. What the Torah calls covenant, Islam calls submission, Hinduism calls ṛta or dharma, and Buddhism calls the Middle Way. Each speaks the grammar of obedience and restoration.

The Qur'an opens this conversation most directly. It acknowledges the Children of Israel as a people uniquely favored by God, yet also accountable for their moral failures.

"O Children of Israel," it says, "remember My favor which I bestowed upon you and that I preferred you above the nations."

Another verse warns that they will cause corruption twice in the earth and afterward be gathered again as one people.

This repetition of dispersion and reunion mirrors the warnings of Deuteronomy 28 and the hope of Deuteronomy 30. Even the Qur'an's vocabulary of law—prayer, charity, truthfulness, and humility—matches the commandments delivered through Moses. In its seventh-century Arabic form, Islam re-states the Hebrew covenant in a global key: the same God, the same moral code, spoken to a wider audience that includes the scattered seed of Israel living among every nation.

Turning eastward, the ancient Vedas of India describe an eternal order called ṛta, the law that holds heaven and earth in balance. "He who upholds ṛta upholds heaven; he who violates it loses the world."

The language is Sanskrit, but the concept is Sinai. Righteousness preserves creation; rebellion unravels it. In later Indian literature, particularly the Bhagavad Gita, the Creator promises to incarnate or intervene whenever this law of truth declines.

"Whenever righteousness declines and unrighteousness rises, I manifest Myself."

This is the same cycle Israel's prophets recorded in historical form—sin, captivity, repentance, redemption—translated here into cosmic philosophy. The Vedas' "noble ones," chosen not by race but by right living, serve the same function as the "kingdom of priests" Moses announced to the Israelites: a people entrusted to keep divine order visible on earth.

Buddhism continues the story from another angle. The Buddha rejected caste and ritual, teaching instead that liberation comes through ethical discipline and compassion. His Eightfold Path—right speech, right action, right livelihood—echoes the social half of the Ten Commandments.

Where the Torah says "Do not bear false witness" and "Do not steal," the Buddha says "Speak truth" and "Take nothing not freely given."

Both paths aim at harmony between inner motive and outer behavior.

In the Dhammapada we read, "Better than a thousand hollow words is one word that brings peace."

That could stand beside the Hebrew proverb, "A word fitly spoken is like apples of gold in pictures of silver."

Even the Buddhist vision of Samsara —the endless repetition of suffering until enlightenment—resembles Israel's repeated exiles until obedience is learned.

The Bodhisattva who vows to suffer on behalf of others is the Eastern reflection of Isaiah's Suffering Servant.

The moral agreement among these scriptures is astonishing. Each insists upon one sovereign Creator or universal principle; each teaches justice above ritual; each celebrates mercy and forgiveness; each demands truth in speech and deed; and each promises restoration after repentance. Across thousands of miles and hundreds of languages, the message remains unchanged: the world is governed by a moral law, and humanity's health depends on keeping it.

Historically, this unity is no mystery. Trade routes linking the Red Sea, Arabia, and India carried not only gold and spices but also stories. Jewish traders in the time of Solomon sailed toward Ophir—probably East Africa or western India—and the tales they told became part of Asia's spiritual vocabulary. Centuries later, when the Axumite empire of Ethiopia controlled ports on both sides of the Red Sea, Israelite, Arab, and Indian merchants exchanged ideas along with goods.

Archaeological inscriptions from South Arabia mention "men of Israel" engaged in trade, and Indian oral histories still speak of shipwrecked strangers who taught the worship of one God. Even the Bene Israel community of

Cochin, India, preserves Hebrew customs and DNA markers identical to those of Middle Eastern Jews and East Africans. The covenant journey clearly extended beyond the Mediterranean world.

Philosophically, the parallels deepen. What Hinduism calls karma, the Torah describes as "you shall reap what you sow." Both recognize moral cause and effect. What Buddhism calls nirvana is identical to the Hebrew shalom — complete peace that arises from harmony with the divine will.

The Sanskrit dharma and the Hebrew Torah both mean "the way," the path of right conduct that holds creation together. Even the names of God converge: El in Hebrew, Ilah in Arabic, and Ila in Sanskrit share the same ancient Semitic root for "the divine." When the Creator speaks, languages differ but essence remains.

Modern scholarship confirms that these moral systems developed in conversation, not isolation.

Anthropologists and theologians alike note that wherever Israelites traveled—Egypt, Arabia, India, Ethiopia—they left behind fragments of their worldview. What began as Torah became Qur'anic law, ṛta, and dharma. The divine melody replayed itself on new instruments. When the

Hebrew prophets said, "The earth shall be full of the knowledge of the Lord," they foresaw precisely this diffusion of truth across borders.

Today's rediscovery of the Hebrew identity among the African diaspora closes the circle. While colonial empires once used religion to divide, the underlying law unites. The Qur'an confirms the Torah, the Vedas anticipate it, and the Sutras echo it. Together they prove that the Creator never allowed His law to perish with any single nation. Even when the Hebrews lost their homeland, their spiritual DNA entered every culture that valued justice, mercy, and humility. The covenant, scattered like seed, took root in every soil.

For the descendants of that covenant awakening now, this realization is not a reason for pride but for perspective. It shows that their restoration will not isolate them from the world but reconcile the world to its Source. When they stand upright in obedience, they harmonize the ancient music of revelation played in Hebrew, Arabic, Sanskrit, and Pali. They become the chord that resolves the dissonance of centuries.

Across all scriptures, the final metaphor is the same: light. The Psalmist wrote, "Thy word is a lamp unto my feet." The Qur'an declares, "Allah is the Light of the heavens and the earth." The Upanishads teach that "the light of all lights shines within the heart," and the Buddha urged, "Be a lamp unto yourselves." Light is the symbol of law, and enlightenment the proof of obedience. When this light rises again among the scattered people and radiates through righteous living, the nations will see one truth in many colors.

The awakening of the Hebrews in our generation therefore completes a universal design. It is the Creator's way of re-tuning the moral universe, drawing every tradition back to its root in the covenant given at Sinai. Malachi foretold, "From the rising of the sun even unto the going down of the same, My name shall be great among the nations." That prophecy is being fulfilled not only in churches or mosques but also in temples and meditation halls, wherever conscience bows to the same eternal law. The world's sacred books are not rivals; they are pages of one story. And the rediscovered children of that story now hold the task of reminding humanity that the Author has never changed.

CHAPTER 5
Empires Of Concealment

Truth is fallen in the street, and equity cannot enter."
— Isaiah 59 : 14

"Nothing is hidden that will not be revealed, nor anything secret that will not be known and come to light." — Luke 8 : 17

1 · The Birth of Erasure

Every empire understands that power begins with narrative. When conquerors rewrite who people are, they no longer need chains; the mind becomes its own cage. The long campaign to sever the descendants of the Hebrews from their identity was therefore not accidental—it was administrative. From Babylon to Rome, from Lisbon to London, the tactic was the same: confiscate the memory, rename the people, and replace revelation with rhetoric.

After the fall of Jerusalem in 70 CE, Rome dispersed surviving Judeans across Africa and Asia. Many merged peacefully into African kingdoms, but imperial historians soon began describing every dark-skinned Semite as "Cushite" or "Ethiopian," erasing distinctions that once defined tribes of Israel. By the time Europe rose from its medieval slumber, Africa had been painted as a continent without covenant or history—fertile land, empty of legacy.

2 · The Vatican and the Veil

When Christianity became Rome's state religion, theology became a tool of control. Councils decided which gospels to canonize and which to burn, ensuring that Rome's image—not Judea's—would shape the faith. Icons were repainted to resemble Europeans; Hebrew feasts were rebranded as Roman holidays. The Passover Lamb became Easter, Shavuot became Pentecost, and the Hebrew calendar disappeared under Julian months.

The early Church Fathers, many sincere, nevertheless helped erase the African and Semitic faces of Scripture. Augustine of Hippo, a North African, taught that salvation made race irrelevant; yet later theologians twisted that idea to claim Africans were cursed. The same empire that had crucified Yeshua now canonized Him in marble whiteness. The veil of the Temple had been torn; Rome sewed it back together.

3 · Cartography as Colonialism

When Portuguese explorers rounded the African coast in the fifteenth century, their maps labeled territories not by nations but by commodities—"Ivory Coast," "Gold Coast," "Slave Coast."

The names themselves denied humanity. Inside those coastal kingdoms lived people who still practiced circumcision, Sabbath rest, and dietary law. European chroniclers saw the customs but refused to record their source. Instead they filed them under "heathen superstition."

Geographers redrew the world to make Europe the center. Even the lines of longitude, running through Greenwich, proclaimed racial hierarchy as scientific fact. Whoever controls the map controls the meaning.

4 · The Economy of Darkness

The Atlantic slave trade was the physical engine of concealment. It not only transported bodies; it trafficked identity. On African shores the names of Yahudah, Levi, and Benjamin were replaced by European surnames that carried no covenant.

The middle passage baptized Hebrews into anonymity. Slave codes forbade reading because literacy leads to lineage. A people who could quote Deuteronomy might one day recognize themselves in it.

In the Americas, plantation preachers were hired to read edited Bibles that skipped every verse promising freedom. The book of Exodus was whispered rather than taught. Yet even in the fields, songs of Moses survived. Oppression silenced the tongue but could not silence the blood.

✡

5 · Science in Service of Supremacy

By the eighteenth century, "race science" replaced theology as the empire's justification. Naturalists such as Carl Linnaeus and Johann Blumenbach cataloged humanity as if it were livestock, arranging skin tones into hierarchies of worth. They called it biology but it was bureaucracy—the management of divine image.

Darwin's later theories of natural selection, though never written as racism, were weaponized by colonial governments to argue that Africans were evolutionary juniors. The irony is cosmic: the same DNA that now proves African Hebrews share ancestry with biblical patriarchs was once used to deny them humanity altogether. The truth hid in the very code misread by its keepers.

6 · Academic Amnesia

Universities followed the empire's lead. Western historians taught that civilization began in Greece, skipping the Egyptian, Nubian, and Semitic sources that taught Greece. Museums displayed African artifacts without mentioning that many bore Hebrew symbols.

Scholars who noticed were marginalized. In the nineteenth century, when explorers in Ethiopia found Falasha Jews and scrolls written in Ge'ez containing the Law of Moses, European journals dismissed them as "Christian heresies."

Textbooks repeated the silence. Generations grew up believing Africa produced slaves, not scholars; tribes, not tribes of Israel. The colonial syllabus became scripture for the modern mind.

7 · The Suppression of Self-Names

Language holds lineage. Empires renamed everything they feared. "Hebrew" became "Negro," "Israelite" became "African," and "slave" became an ethnic category rather than a condition. The term "Black" itself—once a neutral color—

was redefined as a social curse. In legal documents, it denoted property, not personhood. The power of naming turned divine descendants into commercial inventory.

Missionaries often participated unknowingly. Believing they were saving souls, they translated the Bible into local tongues but inserted European imagery and omitted historical context. Converts learned the stories but forgot the protagonists were their own ancestors.

8 · Religion as Re-Branding

Colonial Christianity promised heaven later in exchange for obedience now. It taught the enslaved that their color signified sin and that submission to masters equaled submission to God.

Meanwhile, scriptures describing prophets with woolly hair and bronze skin were reinterpreted as metaphors. When Revelation described Yeshua's feet as "burnished brass," theologians said it symbolized judgment, not complexion.

Islamic empires were not innocent either. Certain dynasties re-labeled indigenous Hebrews of Africa as merely "Sudani," folding them into the general category of the conquered. Both faiths, when politicized, served empire more than enlightenment. Yet both still carried fragments of truth, waiting for rediscovery.

9 · The Paper Crown of Modernity

The Enlightenment promised freedom through reason but merely changed the vocabulary of control. Instead of popes, there were professors; instead of heresy, there was pseudoscience. The colonial archive replaced the Inquisition. Whoever owned the libraries decided what counted as knowledge.

African languages rich with Torah-derived proverbs were dismissed as "oral traditions," unfit for history books. European explorers burned or shipped ancient manuscripts from Timbuktu, labeling them curiosities. The very evidence that could have confirmed Hebrew presence across Africa was hidden in European basements.

10 · The Rebellion of Memory

Despite the censorship, truth survived in fragments: in the songs of field hands, in the proverbs of elders, in the rituals of secret societies that still invoked the Most High by His ancient name. Every whispered "Yah" was an act of rebellion. In the twentieth century, when Pan-African thinkers and Hebrew revivalists compared these fragments, the picture re-formed. Historians like J.A. Rogers, theologians like Rabbi Matthew of Harlem, and scholars of the Lemba and Igbo communities began gathering the pieces empire had scattered. Their reward was ridicule—but also resurrection.

11 · The Age of Exposure

Then came the digital century. Archives once locked behind university walls opened online. DNA testing, dismissed as entertainment, became revelation.

Ordinary people tracing ancestry discovered Levantine and North-African markers hidden in their blood.

The internet made censorship impossible. Every new discovery echoed the same refrain: the descendants of the covenant had survived every empire that tried to erase them.

Museums quietly revised exhibits; academic journals cautiously admitted "unexpected genetic continuities." What prophets proclaimed by vision, scientists now confirmed by data. The veil of silence began to tear.

12 · The Falling of the Walls

Empires fall not when armies invade but when lies collapse. The revelation of Hebrew identity among people once called African-American is not merely ethnic awakening—it is prophetic justice. It exposes the spiritual bankruptcy of systems built on deception. The Church must confront its whitening of scripture; universities must correct their Eurocentric chronologies; governments must recognize that those they enslaved were heirs of the very covenant that shaped Western law.

This unveiling terrifies institutions because it redistributes authority. If the once-enslaved are the covenant bearers, then the moral center of history shifts south and west, away from the marble halls of empire toward the people who survived its lash.

13 · Truth as Liberation

Every revelation begins with discomfort. The Hebrews in Egypt first realized they were captive before they could cry for deliverance. Likewise, modern descendants must face the depth of manipulation before they can reclaim their heritage. To know that your ancestors were renamed, repainted, and rewritten is painful—but it is also power. Pain uncovers purpose.

The same scripture that predicted scattering also promised gathering. "I will restore your judges as at the first," said the prophet Isaiah. Restoration requires memory. Each rediscovered manuscript, each corrected history lesson, is a brick in the rebuilding of Zion—not the geographic hill, but the spiritual nation spread across continents.

14 · The Unmasking of Power

As more people awaken, the machinery of misinformation sputters. Students challenge textbooks; pastors replace portraits; archaeologists re-examine artifacts once labeled "African fetishes" and now recognize menorah patterns and Hebrew inscriptions. The system that thrived on ignorance cannot survive education. Light dissolves darkness by existing, not by arguing.

The empires of concealment crumble because truth requires no permission to live. It merely waits for the appointed generation to open its eyes.

15 · The Return of the Record

In our time, the lost record returns home. Scrolls once buried in desert caves resurface; digital libraries restore banned texts; and the descendants of the covenant translate them anew in their own voices. Knowledge is migrating back to its rightful heirs. The world calls it scholarship; heaven calls it prophecy fulfilled.

What began as theft ends as testimony. The same systems that hid the truth now unwittingly reveal it through technology and transparency. What empires meant for erasure becomes evidence. History bows to prophecy once again.

✡

16 · The End of Concealment

The Creator allowed concealment to test character. Had the truth been obvious, righteousness would have been cheap. By surviving centuries of distortion and still seeking the Most High, the scattered children proved worthy of the revelation. Now, as the walls fall, they must not rebuild them in reverse by exalting flesh over faith. The purpose of uncovering is unity, not superiority.

The book of Daniel promised that knowledge would increase at the end of the age. That increase is not merely technological; it is spiritual recollection. The empire's age of deception has expired. The age of remembrance has begun.

"And the books were opened." — Daniel 7 : 10

The empire wrote its version of the story; the covenant people will write the last chapter.

CHAPTER 6
The Great Awakening & The Modern Signs

"In the last days, knowledge shall increase and many shall run to and fro." — Daniel 12 : 4

"When the Spirit of Truth comes, He will guide you into all truth." — John 16 : 13

1 · From Whisper to Worldwide Voice

For centuries the truth about the scattered covenant people existed like a candle hidden under a bowl—its light faint, its smoke contained. Then, without warning, the world began to change. The same technologies once used to deceive now became the very instruments of disclosure.

The internet, designed for commerce and entertainment, turned into a digital Sinai where long-buried testimonies reappeared in every tongue. Ordinary men and women tracing their ancestry discovered genetic markers linking them to ancient Israel. Elders who once feared ridicule spoke openly. A movement without headquarters or hierarchy began to rise. It did not wait for permission; it spread like dawn.

The prophets foresaw this moment. They described a generation who would "remember themselves in the land of their captivity." That remembering is the true definition of awakening—not political rebellion but spiritual return. The world calls it identity politics; heaven calls it repentance.

✡

2 · The Prophetic Timeline Revisited

The first recorded slave ship carrying captive Israelites arrived in Virginia in 1619. Four centuries later, in 2019, global attention suddenly shifted to questions of justice, heritage, and restitution.

The timing startled even skeptics, for Genesis 15 : 13–14 had foretold a 400-year period of servitude followed by deliverance. Whether one interprets this literally or symbolically, the rhythm of history aligned with prophecy. After four hundred years of silence, the descendants began to speak—and the world listened.

These parallels are not coincidence; they are the calendar of the Covenant Keeper. Empires rise and fall by design. What seems political or social is, beneath the surface, spiritual choreography moving toward restoration.

✡

3 · Signs in Science and Society

Every new scientific discovery now affirms an ancient scripture. DNA analysis, linguistic reconstruction, and archaeology continue to close the gap between belief and proof. Even climate patterns echo prophetic imagery: rivers drying where empires once stood, deserts blooming where exile began. Humanity calls it global change; prophets called it the birth pangs of renewal.

Culturally, too, signs multiply. Artists, scholars, and youth across continents return to ancestral languages and names once forbidden. They wear symbols of covenant not as fashion but as testimony. The revival of Hebrew phrases such as Shalom, Yah, and Todah among people of the diaspora is not trend—it is memory resurfacing through generations who never studied the language yet instinctively pronounce it. Spirit remembers what schooling forgets.

4 · Technology as Trumpet

The ancient shofar summoned Israel to gather; today the call travels through fiber optics and satellites. Live-streamed lessons, documentaries, and social platforms carry the message farther than any missionary could. One post reaches thousands; one revelation becomes a chain of rediscovery. The same networks that once broadcast confusion now carry prophecy. Truth has gone viral.

This transformation fulfills another promise: that the gospel of the kingdom would be preached in all nations before the end. The "good news" is not a denomination—it is the announcement that the covenant still stands, that the scattered are still loved, and that obedience still brings blessing. Technology simply amplifies the ancient sound of grace.

5 · The Awakening Within

The greatest sign is not external but internal. Across the diaspora, people who never met share identical dreams—visions of ancient cities, deserts, and temples. Children speak of being from places their families never heard of. Hearts ache for justice but also for holiness. This is spiritual DNA activating, the soul's way of confirming what the body already carries.

Awakening begins when individuals reject shame and reclaim purpose. To know you are Hebrew is not to boast of ancestry but to accept assignment. It means to practice the law of love, to forgive, to restore. The awakening demands moral transformation as much as historical recognition. Otherwise identity becomes idolatry.

6 · The Unity of the Scattered

The Most High designed dispersion to guarantee diversity. Each region that received the Hebrews added a piece of its culture to the covenant mosaic. In West Africa the music kept rhythm with psalms; in the Caribbean the drums echoed temple cadence; in America the spirituals preserved prophecy; in Ethiopia and South Africa the festivals endured.

Now these fragments return to one another like puzzle pieces drawn by magnetism. When they meet, none is superior; each holds a key the other lost.

Unity does not erase difference; it harmonizes it. The awakening teaches that family means variety under one Father. The proof that the Hebrews are rising again is not their agreement on every doctrine but their refusal to hate each other for disagreement.

7 · Dreams of Deliverance

Movements of liberation always begin with imagination. Moses saw the burning bush before he saw the Red Sea open. Likewise, the present generation dreams of nations rebuilt on righteousness—schools teaching both scripture and science, economies guided by ethics, governance measured by mercy. These visions are not utopian; they are the logical next step in revelation. Every empire collapses; only covenant communities endure.

The prophets described this renewal as the desert blossoming. The barren lands of forgotten identity now bloom with purpose. What was called "minority" becomes majority in moral influence, because truth commands attention even without armies.

8 · The Resistance to Revelation

Awakening never arrives without opposition. Institutions that profited from ignorance resist exposure. Media labels truth as extremism; academia calls faith myth. Yet suppression only spreads the message. The more critics argue, the more seekers investigate. This paradox is divine strategy: persecution as publicity.

Those who awaken must therefore walk wisely. The goal is not revenge but revelation. Anger can ignite, but only love can sustain. The awakening's credibility rests on character; the new nation must act with the dignity empire denied it.

9 · The Return of Prophecy

Old prophecies read like today's headlines. Isaiah spoke of people "coming out of darkness," and Ezekiel envisioned dry bones rising.

Those bones are the descendants of the diaspora—once dismembered, now re-membered into purpose.

Jeremiah promised that the covenant would be written on hearts, not stone; and indeed, the new tablets are internal.

People across cultures feel conviction without clergy. They are taught by Spirit more than by institutions. The same breath that animated Adam now awakens his heirs.

10 · Modern Signs in Every Field

In medicine, scientists discover that stress from generational trauma alters DNA—a physical confirmation of Deuteronomy's statement that the sins of the fathers affect the children. In economics, nations built on exploitation crumble under debt, fulfilling the law that unjust scales bring ruin. In politics, hidden corruption surfaces daily, echoing the warning that what is whispered in darkness will be shouted from rooftops.

Even astronomy contributes: telescopes reveal galaxies ordered by proportion, mirroring the Torah's design of measurements and sabbaths. The universe keeps covenant better than its custodians.

All creation testifies that a new order approaches, one founded on truth rather than empire. The scattered must be ready not only to rejoice in identity but to govern by righteousness when restoration comes.

✡

11 · The Moral Responsibility of Knowledge

To awaken is to inherit obligation. Knowing the truth without living it breeds hypocrisy. The Hebrews were not chosen for privilege but for service. The modern descendant must therefore embody honesty in business, purity in family, and compassion in community.

Each act of integrity repairs what centuries of deceit destroyed. The world will believe the revelation not because of eloquent arguments but because awakened people live as evidence.

The Most High does not awaken a people to make them celebrities; He awakens them to make them caretakers of justice. This is the covenant's fine print: identity is not ownership—it is stewardship.

12 · Signs in the Heavens and the Heart

Prophets used cosmic language to describe moral events. "The sun shall be darkened, the stars shall fall." In our time, eclipses, earthquakes, and celestial alignments fascinate scientists but also stir the spirit.

They remind humanity that heaven still signals earth. Yet the greatest sign is emotional rather than astronomical: compassion increasing where cruelty once ruled, reconciliation between divided families, the hunger for truth among youth who reject cynicism. These are miracles measured not in miles but in mercy.

13 · From Identity to Inheritance

Recognition of heritage is only the first door. Beyond it lies the inheritance of purpose: to rebuild societies on divine principles. This includes education rooted in wisdom, economies balanced by fairness, and art guided by beauty rather than vanity.

When the awakened live creatively and ethically, they display the glory of the covenant. The world will see in them not a slogan but a solution.

14 · The Global Ripple

Across continents, nations outside the diaspora begin to notice. Scholars in Asia study the Hebrew roots of African traditions; musicians in Europe sample psalms in new rhythms; spiritual seekers in Latin America identify with Israel's struggle for liberation.

The awakening of one people sparks moral awakening in many. The covenant, once localized, becomes planetary. This is the hidden purpose of scattering—to seed conscience worldwide so that when truth blooms, the earth already knows the song.

15 · The Final Sign

The final sign of awakening is peace. When those once oppressed can forgive without forgetting, when they can teach rather than retaliate, when they can stand in dignity without demanding dominance, the prophecy is fulfilled.

The scattered have become the light they sought. The curse has become curriculum. History bends back toward holiness.

The Most High does not awaken a people merely to tell them who they were, but to reveal who He still is. The same hand that allowed dispersion now gathers His children through knowledge, unity, and love. The world watches, not realizing it is witnessing scripture continue to write itself.

"Arise, shine; for thy light is come, and the glory of the LORD is risen upon thee." — Isaiah 60 : 1

The awakening is no longer a rumor. It is reality. It lives in data and in dreams, in cities and in villages, in every heart that dares to remember. The lost have found themselves, and in doing so, they have found their God again.

CHAPTER 7
The Gathering Of Nations & The Return To Law

"And it shall come to pass in the last days that many peoples shall go and say, Come, let us go up to the mountain of the LORD, and He will teach us His ways, and we will walk in His paths." — Isaiah 2 : 2-3

"And I saw another angel flying in mid-heaven, having the everlasting gospel to proclaim unto them that dwell on the earth, and to every nation, and kindred, and tongue, and people." — Revelation 14 : 6

1 · From Awakening to Assembly

Every revelation eventually demands organization. A seed that germinates must take form; otherwise its growth becomes chaos. After centuries of dispersion, the descendants of the covenant are awakening not merely as individuals but as an assembly drawn from every corner of the earth.

The prophets described this phenomenon as the gathering of nations. It is not a geopolitical summit but a spiritual migration—souls traveling toward one moral mountain.

The Hebrew awakening cannot remain a private epiphany. It must translate into communal ethics, shared structure, and collective responsibility. The return to law begins when awakened people learn again to live by principle instead of impulse, by covenant rather than convenience.

✡

2 · The Pattern of Regathering

The Most High always gathers by stages. When Israel left Egypt, the first command was to assemble at Sinai to receive instruction.

Likewise, the scattered today are called first to knowledge, then to unity, and finally to nationhood of conscience. The new exodus does not involve crossing deserts but crossing divisions.

The gathering occurs wherever truth becomes the meeting place—homes transformed into study circles, online platforms turned into sanctuaries, communities rebuilding schools rooted in both scripture and science. This is the new wilderness, where order replaces confusion and covenant replaces culture shock.

✡

3 · The Law Re-written on Hearts

Jeremiah foretold a covenant not engraved on stone but written on human hearts. The return to law therefore begins within. Obedience born of fear produces tyranny, but obedience born of love restores balance.

As the Spirit inscribes divine statutes into conscience, people begin to live righteously without external policing. This is the maturity the prophets longed for—a world where morality becomes instinct because truth has become identity.

Such transformation dismantles the myth that law and liberty oppose each other. The Torah's purpose was never to imprison but to instruct. The righteous man is not enslaved by commandment; he is liberated by clarity.

4 · Healing the Divided Family

The gathering of nations begins with reconciliation among the scattered tribes themselves. Centuries of oppression planted suspicion between brothers—continent against continent, religion against religion, hue against hue.

But the awakening reveals that diversity was part of design. The tribe in the Caribbean, the clan in America, the community in Africa, and the fellowship in Europe are limbs of one body rediscovering motion. Forgiveness is the circulation that keeps that body alive.

True regathering will therefore sound less like political unification and more like family reunion—a recognition that disagreement need not mean disinheritance. When we honor the different paths by which the Creator preserved us, we rebuild the house of Israel plank by plank.

✡

5 · The Law as Universal Blueprint

Every nation hungers for justice but quarrels about its definition. The Torah provides an eternal template: equality before the law, compassion for the poor, protection of the stranger, rest for laborers, stewardship of land, and honest trade.

These principles, though ancient, remain the only sustainable constitution for humanity. The gathering of nations is not a theocracy imposed by force but a voluntary alignment with this blueprint.

When governments codify mercy and honesty into policy, when economics honors sabbath rest for both soil and worker, when education cultivates reverence for life, the return to law has begun. The covenant's goal is civilization, not ceremony.

6 · From Religion to Righteousness

The age of denominational rivalry is ending. The Most High did not awaken the scattered to found more sects but to demonstrate morality without manipulation.

The gathered nation will not be measured by temples built but by lives repaired. Worship will be defined less by ritual performance and more by ethical excellence.

The prophets warned that sacrifices without justice offend Heaven; the new Israel must therefore build systems where truth governs daily commerce and compassion governs leadership.

When a people lives ethically, their very existence becomes evangelism. Righteousness is the only sermon the world still believes.

7 · Justice and Economy

The ancient Jubilee commanded release of debts every fiftieth year. This economic law preserved equality and prevented permanent poverty. Its revival is essential for global healing. Modern capitalism's endless appetite mirrors

Pharaoh's brick quotas—labor without rest, accumulation without compassion. The return to law will reintroduce balance: profit with purpose, innovation without exploitation, production guided by gratitude.

Communities embracing covenant economics will thrive because fairness is fertile soil. When transactions honor dignity, wealth circulates instead of corrupting. This is not idealism; it is divine mathematics.

✡

8 · Education as Priesthood

In ancient Israel, Levites taught as well as served. In the modern restoration, every educator becomes a Levite of truth. Schools must return to their sacred function—to cultivate wisdom rather than indoctrination.

Children must learn that mathematics reflects order, that science explores creation, that art celebrates the image of God. When education reunites intellect with spirit, nations regenerate minds instead of manufacturing workers.

Knowledge divorced from morality built the empires of concealment; knowledge wedded to virtue will build the kingdom of light.

✡

9 · Women and the Restoration of Balance

Throughout exile, women preserved faith when institutions failed. They sang psalms over cradles, protected oral history, and kept hope alive. The gathering honors them not as auxiliaries but as anchors.

Scripture portrays Wisdom herself in feminine form; without her, no law stands. Therefore, the return to law includes restoring honor to mothers, scholars, and leaders who embody the nurturing justice of the Most High. A nation that silences its women silences half its prophecy.

10 · Inter-Nations and Allies

The gathering of nations does not exclude the rest of humanity. Isaiah foresaw Gentiles joining hands with Israel to rebuild ruins. Every sincere heart that embraces truth becomes part of the covenant's expansion.

The world need not convert to Hebrew identity; it need only submit to Hebrew ethics—the law of love and integrity that undergirds all true religion. Thus the awakening of one people becomes the conscience of all.

11 · Modern Israel and the Moral Mirror

The existence of a political state called Israel confuses many. The covenant people must remember that geography alone does not equal prophecy. The modern nation fulfills part of restoration but not its completion; righteousness, not real estate, is the true promised land.

When both the land's inhabitants and the dispersed descendants pursue justice and mercy, the prophecy will find balance. Until then, every people of faith carries a fragment of Zion within their character.

12 · The Return to Sabbath Rhythm

The Sabbath embodies the entire covenant principle: creation, rest, and remembrance. In a world addicted to motion, rediscovering sacred rhythm is revolutionary. Rest restores sanity, gratitude, and equality.

When all nations adopt rhythms of renewal—time for family, reflection, and restraint—they unconsciously fulfill the law. The gathering is not merely physical; it is temporal. Humanity is learning to breathe again in divine time.

13 · The Covenant Flag

Every people rallies around a symbol. For the restored Hebrews, the true flag is not a political banner but the commandments themselves.

They are stripes of light representing truth, compassion, discipline, faith, humility, honesty, and peace.

When these virtues fly over our conduct, the world will recognize the covenant without any need for declaration. The law becomes visible when lived.

14 · Resistance and Reform

The return to law will face hostility from systems built on exploitation. Those profiting from chaos will accuse order of oppression. But history favors endurance. Empires of deceit cannot outlast communities of integrity.

The awakened must reform quietly but persistently— building businesses that model fairness, governments that refuse bribery, media that honors truth. The revolution of righteousness advances one ethical choice at a time.

15 · The Final Gathering

Prophecy concludes with a vision of nations flowing to one mountain, their weapons reforged into tools of cultivation. This image is not fantasy; it is the Creator's blueprint for civilization. When humanity finally values life above dominance, the scattering ends.

The Hebrew people, once despised, will serve as mediators of peace, teaching law through example. In that day the phrase "chosen people" will mean "chosen to serve."

The Great Gathering is not evacuation but evolution— the flowering of a promise that began with Abraham and now blossoms through his far-flung descendants. The law they restore will heal what empire destroyed. And when the earth is governed by compassion rather than conquest, the covenant will have completed its circle.

"For out of Zion shall go forth the law, and the word of the LORD from Jerusalem." — Micah 4 : 2

The nations are already moving toward that mountain—one act of justice, one word of truth, one reconciled heart at a time. The return to law has begun, and with it, the end of captivity.

CHAPTER 8
The Return Of The Name &
The Voice Of The Covenant

"Therefore My people shall know My name; therefore they shall know in that day that I am He that doth speak: behold, it is I." — Isaiah 52 : 6

"And I will give to the people a pure language, that they may all call upon the name of the LORD, to serve Him with one consent." — Zephaniah 3 : 9

1 · The Silenced Name

When Israel fell and empires rose, the first thing they buried was the Name. Language holds power, and no word carries greater energy than the true Name of the Creator.

Over centuries, translation and tradition replaced the personal name Yah or Yahuwah with titles like Lord and God. The substitution seemed harmless, yet it quietly disconnected worshipers from intimacy.

A title is public; a name is personal. When the Name disappeared, relationship became religion.

The prophets mourned this loss. Jeremiah recorded the divine lament, "My people have forgotten My name for

Baal." The word Baal means master — proof that even devotion without discernment can become bondage.

To call upon "the Lord" without knowing which lord one serves is to speak into echo. The scattering of the people scattered the pronunciation, but the covenant preserved the memory. The rediscovery of the Name is therefore not novelty; it is homecoming.

✡

2 · The Meaning of Yah

The Hebrew Yah derives from the verb hayah — to be, to exist. When the Creator told Moses, "I AM THAT I AM," He revealed Himself as existence itself, the breath behind every breath. The short form Yah appears throughout the Psalms: Hallelu-Yah means "praise be to the One Who Is." This is not merely linguistic curiosity; it is theology condensed into a syllable. To speak His Name is to acknowledge that life itself depends on His being.

In exile, this Name survived hidden in song. Enslaved Africans, descended from those same covenant people, chanted "Yah" in spirituals and invocations even when forbidden to read. Without realizing it, they kept the ancient vibration alive. Now, as consciousness rises, that vibration returns to its rightful clarity.

3 · The Power of Pronunciation

Every language shapes thought; every sound carries frequency. In Hebrew, the letters of the sacred Name correspond to the sound of breath itself — Yod-Heh-Waw-Heh. When whispered, it forms no hard consonants, only the inhaling and exhaling of life. The first cry of a newborn and the last sigh of the dying both pronounce His Name. All living creatures speak it without speech. This revelation shows why He told Moses, "This is My name forever, and this is My memorial unto all generations." The Name endures because existence cannot forget its Source.

To rediscover the pronunciation is not about phonetic precision but about reverent awareness. Whether one says Yah, Yahuah, Jehovah, or Elohim, the heart must mean The One Who Is. Sound without spirit is noise; spirit without sound is silence. The true invocation unites both.

4 · The Voice of the People

Just as the divine Name returns, so does the collective voice of the covenant people. For centuries others interpreted Scripture for them, translated their heritage into foreign idioms, and spoke about them rather than with them. Now the heirs of the prophets speak for themselves again.

They read Torah in the languages of the diaspora, sing psalms with ancestral rhythm, and preach justice with the fire of experience. This is prophecy reincarnated in plain speech. The voice that empire silenced rises in harmony, not in hatred.

The true prophetic voice does not curse nations; it calls them higher. It does not predict destruction for pleasure but pleads for righteousness. When the scattered Hebrews regain that voice, they fulfill the purpose of their election—to be light-bearers, not lightning-throwers.

5 · The Restoration of Language

Zephaniah's promise of a "pure language" foretold more than grammar. Purity means clarity—speech cleansed of confusion. As more people study Hebrew, Aramaic, and related tongues, ancient meanings reappear. Words long mistranslated reveal fresh power: shalom meaning wholeness rather than mere peace, emunah meaning faithfulness rather than blind belief, tzedakah meaning justice expressed through generosity.

When the covenant people learn to speak with precision, they begin to think with precision, and truth replaces superstition.

Linguistic revival also bridges continents. Diaspora communities learning Hebrew reconnect naturally with African Semitic languages such as Amharic and Tigrinya, realizing they were never foreign.

The family of tongues proves the family of blood. The language of heaven, once exiled, is finding its earthly hosts again.

6 · The Sacred Name in Other Faiths

The divine Name never vanished entirely; it migrated through other traditions. In Islam, the word Allah preserves the Semitic root Elah, meaning "The God." In Sanskrit hymns, the term Ya or Yah occasionally appears as an exclamation of divinity.

Even in the hymns of ancient Egypt, the phrase Iah described the lunar light of the Creator. These linguistic footprints confirm that humanity never forgot entirely—it only pronounced differently.

Therefore, the rediscovery of the Name should not produce division but recognition. Each language held a fragment of the lost harmony. The returning Hebrews gather those fragments into one sound, restoring the melody of creation.

✡

7 · The Ethical Voice of the Covenant

To speak the Name without living its law is hypocrisy. The true return of the Name requires the return of righteousness.

The covenant's voice must resound through behavior—through honesty in trade, purity in relationships, compassion toward the oppressed, and reverence in daily speech.

When people of the covenant live by these principles, every word they utter becomes sacred because it harmonizes with the Name they bear.

This is why the commandment forbids taking the Name "in vain." It is not about pronunciation but about representation.

Whoever carries the divine reputation must live accordingly. The awakening generation must therefore become living translations of holiness.

✡

8 · Music and the Renewed Sound

Throughout exile, the drum and the hymn preserved covenant rhythm. Now that identity is returning, music itself transforms. Modern Hebrew choirs, African praise bands, gospel ensembles, and reggae prophets all channel the same pulse. The Spirit conducts them into symphony.

The prophecy of Amos comes alive: "In that day will I raise up the tabernacle of David."

The rebuilding begins in song before it appears in stone.

Sound shapes atmosphere. When communities sing the divine Name with sincerity, neighborhoods change. Depression lifts. Violence subsides. The vibration of praise repairs what speeches cannot. The covenant voice is melody married to morality.

9 · The Prophetic Return of Authority

In Scripture, to speak in the Name of Yah was to act with His authority. Prophets did not rely on titles or institutions; their credential was obedience. Today, that mantle is being restored—not to celebrity preachers or political figures, but to ordinary men and women whose integrity grants them credibility.

They are the modern Nehemiahs rebuilding walls of conscience, the Deborahs judging with wisdom, the Jeremiahs weeping for nations. Their authority is humility. Their platform is purity.

As these voices rise, the world rediscovers what true leadership sounds like—firm yet compassionate, passionate yet peaceful. The return of the Name includes the return of voices worthy to bear it.

10 · The Name and the Nations

The prophets declared that all nations would ultimately call on one Name. This does not mean uniform religion but unified reverence.

Christians who honor Yahshua, Muslims who submit to Allah, Hindus who seek Param-Atman, and Buddhists who pursue enlightenment all move toward the same Source when they live by truth and love.

The covenant people's task is to clarify, not to condemn—to reveal the origin of every righteous impulse and invite all hearts to return to the One who breathed life into them.

The return of the Name is therefore also the return of peace, for when humanity worships one Creator in spirit and in truth, rivalry loses its reason.

11 · The Healing Power of Calling

Modern science confirms what faith always knew: spoken words affect matter. Vibrations alter molecular structures; positive speech accelerates healing. When believers call upon the divine Name with faith, they align their biology with creation's original frequency.

Illness often yields to such harmony because the body recognizes its Composer. The Name becomes medicine—the syllables of existence restoring existence.

This understanding does not dismiss medicine; it completes it. The same Creator who designed DNA designed sound as therapy. To invoke His Name with sincerity is to participate in the physics of faith.

12 · The Return of Sacred Speech

Every culture once held speech sacred. Oaths were binding because words were considered creative forces. Modern society, obsessed with chatter, treats language as disposable.

The restoration of the covenant re-sanctifies speech. Truth-telling becomes worship; gossip becomes profanity.

To speak with purpose is to imitate the Creator who said, "Let there be light." Each conversation becomes a miniature creation.

When a people reclaim the holiness of their own words, they no longer need external censorship. The mouth becomes altar; the tongue, priest.

13 · The Sound of Unity

As the scattered tribes learn again to call upon the same Name, the prophecy of Zephaniah begins to unfold: a pure language uniting all peoples. The accents differ, but the intention harmonizes.

Whether pronounced in Yoruba cadence, Caribbean rhythm, or American tone, the syllable Yah crosses boundaries like breath crossing lungs. The unity of language births the unity of purpose. The covenant people, once a question mark in history, become an exclamation point in destiny.

14 · The Everlasting Name

Scripture ends where it began—with the Name. "From the rising of the sun to its setting, My Name shall be great among the nations."

That promise outlasted every empire. Pharaoh could not drown it, Rome could not rename it, and slavery could not silence it. Now it returns carried in the mouths of those once silenced. The world that once mocked their cries will soon echo their praise.

The return of the Name is the return of truth, the return of breath, the return of belonging. It is the sound of chains breaking—not by force but by remembrance.

When the covenant people call on Yah with clean hearts and righteous hands, heaven answers not with thunder but with recognition. The Father knows His children by voice.

"This people have I formed for Myself; they shall show forth My praise." — Isaiah 43 : 21

The Name has come home. And with it, the world begins to breathe again.

CHAPTER 9
The New Jerusalem: Building The Kingdom On Earth

"And I John saw the holy city, new Jerusalem, coming down from God out of heaven, prepared as a bride adorned for her husband." — Revelation 21 : 2

"Thy kingdom come, Thy will be done in earth, as it is in heaven." — Matthew 6 : 10

1 · Vision Made Visible

Every prophecy ends with a city. Not a metropolis of steel and concrete, but a society shaped by holiness. The New Jerusalem is not a destination floating in the clouds; it is a design descending into conscience.

It represents the moment when humanity's architecture finally mirrors Heaven's order—when justice, mercy, and truth are built into streets, schools, and marketplaces.

The scattered Hebrews were never meant to vanish into history; they were meant to return as builders. The awakened generation stands where Moses once stood, seeing the promised order from afar and called to enter by faith and labor.

2 · Heaven as a Blueprint

Scripture describes the New Jerusalem with measurements precise enough for engineers and artists alike: square foundations, transparent gold streets, gates of pearl. These are symbols of moral geometry.

The square signifies equality; the gold, purity; the transparency, honesty. Every material reflects virtue. The design instructs that a righteous nation must be mathematically fair and spiritually beautiful.

To build such a kingdom on earth requires more than monuments; it requires mindsets. The cornerstone is character. Every citizen becomes a brick; every good deed, mortar. Walls of salvation rise only where people choose integrity.

3 · Economy of Equity

The Kingdom's economy rejects both greed and dependency. It restores the balance of giving and receiving known as tzedakah—righteous generosity. In the New Jerusalem model, wealth circulates like blood, carrying life to every limb of society. Business becomes ministry; labor regains dignity. A worker's wage honors both skill and soul.

Instead of corporations devouring communities, communities cultivate enterprises that feed justice. Land is not hoarded but stewarded; food systems respect earth's sabbath.

The modern descendant of the covenant must pioneer models of cooperative ownership, transparent trade, and ethical technology. These are not new inventions but resurrections of Mosaic principles.

4 · Government by Conscience

In the Kingdom, leadership is service. Thrones become tools. The judge, prophet, and mayor merge into one calling: guardian of fairness. Laws reflect divine ethics rather than party agendas.

Decisions are measured not by profit margins but by moral impact. The best leader is the one who listens most deeply to the quiet law written in the heart.

When power is purified by purpose, governance becomes worship. The world has tried monarchy, democracy, and oligarchy; the New Jerusalem introduces theocracy by conscience—each soul ruled from within by the Spirit of Truth.

5 · Education as Eden

Knowledge was the first gift humanity abused and must be the first garden restored. Schools in the New Jerusalem teach wisdom before information.

Children learn the history of covenant alongside mathematics, languages, and ecology. Science no longer wars with faith; both walk hand in hand discovering how creation functions so that it can be honored, not exploited.

Art is consecrated again, showing beauty as a form of truth rather than vanity.

Education ceases to be competition for degrees and becomes cultivation of destiny. Each child learns not what to think but how to think with holiness.

6 · The Healing of Nations

Revelation 22 describes leaves from the tree of life "for the healing of the nations." That tree grows wherever forgiveness takes root. The New Jerusalem society cannot be built on resentment; it rises only on reconciliation.

Former enemies become partners in purpose. The children of colonizers and the children of the enslaved must rebuild the world together, not in guilt but in grace.

Healing also means repairing systems that poison body and spirit—reforming healthcare to value prevention, food to serve wellness, and media to nourish truth. Every healed person becomes a healer; every restored family becomes medicine to its neighborhood.

7 · Technology in Service to Truth

Tools are neutral until motives corrupt them. The Kingdom transforms technology from distraction into devotion. Devices designed for vanity become instruments of virtue—archives of wisdom, networks of compassion, classrooms without walls.

Artificial intelligence becomes applied intelligence when it teaches empathy rather than exploitation. Innovation bows to inspiration.

The Hebrew heritage of craftsmanship—seen in Bezalel who built the Tabernacle—continues through inventors who code with conscience. The New Jerusalem shines not because of neon lights but because knowledge serves holiness.

8 · The Covenant Family

At the heart of the Kingdom stands family, the original temple. Marriage regains its sanctity as partnership in purpose; parenthood becomes priesthood. The home again hosts prayer, study, and laughter.

Communities thrive when households honor covenant. The collapse of family during exile created social ruin; its restoration will create national redemption. The New Jerusalem begins at the dinner table.

9 · Cultural Renewal

Culture is collective memory expressed in art, language, and lifestyle. In exile it was distorted by survival; in the Kingdom it becomes celebration.

Music, fashion, and literature no longer imitate empire but interpret eternity.

Artists see themselves as prophets with paintbrushes; architects design according to harmony and light.

Every festival, from harvest to new moon, honors both ancestry and divinity. Joy becomes policy.

10 · Justice and Mercy Kissing

David sang of the day when justice and mercy would kiss. That union defines the New Jerusalem. Courts will still exist, but punishment gives way to restoration.

The aim is not revenge but repentance. A society that heals wrongdoers while protecting the innocent mirrors the divine heart.

The law is firm yet compassionate, strong yet forgiving. It corrects without crushing.

Such justice requires citizens who understand mercy as strength, not weakness. Only hearts acquainted with suffering can legislate with empathy.

The descendants of the oppressed are therefore uniquely qualified to build systems that balance both scales.

11 · The Temple Without Walls

John's vision concludes, "I saw no temple therein, for the Lord God Almighty and the Lamb are the temple." This means worship becomes a way of life. Every marketplace transaction, every handshake, every invention becomes liturgy.

The distinction between sacred and secular dissolves. The presence of the Most High fills daily labor like incense fills a sanctuary. Humanity at last lives as priesthood—constant communion through conduct.

When holiness occupies ordinary spaces, the world itself becomes temple. That is the meaning of the Kingdom on earth.

✡

12 · The Role of the Awakened People

The Hebrews reborn in the diaspora carry the blueprint because they have lived both captivity and compassion.

Their assignment is to teach justice through experience, to model humility forged by hardship.

They are not crowned over the world but commissioned to serve it.

Their songs of survival become instruction manuals for nations lost in arrogance.

The once-despised stone becomes the cornerstone of civilization.

The new kingdom will not rise through conquest but through consistency—families choosing truth over convenience, communities choosing cooperation over competition, leaders choosing service over self.

Every such choice lays another brick in Jerusalem's invisible walls.

13 · Heaven Touching Earth

When these principles are practiced, heaven and earth overlap. Prayer and policy become synonyms. Angels and humans labor in the same direction. The dream that drove prophets to tears finally solidifies into reality: a planet healed by obedience.

The glow John saw descending from the sky was not radiation but revelation—the brilliance of people living in divine order.

The New Jerusalem is therefore not postponed; it is under construction. Every act of kindness, every fair law, every forgiven offense adds another gemstone to its foundation.

14 · The City of Light

In that city, there is no need for the sun because truth itself illuminates. Lies have no market there; deceit finds no buyer. Children play without fear; elders die without regret. Nations bring their glory into it not as trophies but as tributes.

Diversity becomes the spectrum of divine creativity. The covenant people, once divided by distance and doctrine, now shine as one collective lamp whose flame is love.

15 · The Invitation

The Revelation closes with an invitation: "The Spirit and the Bride say, Come." That call still echoes. The New Jerusalem welcomes every soul willing to live by truth, regardless of ancestry.

The Hebrew awakening is not a gated community but an open door into righteousness. The requirement is not lineage but loyalty—to the law of love, to the rhythm of justice, to the harmony of peace. Whoever answers becomes citizen of the Kingdom.

"Blessed are they that do His commandments, that they may have right to the tree of life, and may enter in through the gates into the city." — Revelation 22 : 14

The city is rising. Its foundations are already laid in the hearts of the awakened. Every truthful word, every merciful act, every reconciled relationship adds another beam of light to its skyline.

The Kingdom of Heaven is not distant; it is developing within you. And when the righteous rule through compassion, when the humble govern through wisdom, the earth itself will declare: The New Jerusalem has come.

CHAPTER 10
The Crown Of Glory & The Age Of Peace

I have said these things for years, on sidewalks and street corners, in church parking lots and living rooms, sometimes to applause, sometimes to silence.

And still I say them, because the truth does not grow tired. It waits—like the sunrise—whether or not we open our eyes. This final word is not a conclusion but a continuation. The book may end here; the awakening will not.

1. Why I Keep Speaking

People ask, "Why do you keep saying the same thing?"

Because every day I meet someone who has never heard it. Because every generation risks forgetting what the last one learned. Because the system that benefits from our confusion never sleeps, and therefore the messenger cannot either.

When I say, "You are Hebrew," I am not making noise—I am announcing identity.

It is a trumpet blast, a wake-up call to a people lulled by entertainment and exhaustion. Some grow weary of the sound, but the alarm keeps ringing until the house wakes. Once you understand that, repetition becomes reverence.

2. The Weight of Calling

This message cost me comfort. It cost me invitations, friendships, and at times safety. But obedience outweighs acceptance. I was not chosen to be popular; I was chosen to be persistent. The Most High placed a word in my spirit that burns even when I try to silence it.

Calling is a heavy coat in summer—it makes you sweat, but you cannot take it off. To speak truth in an age of lies is to stand in the middle of traffic waving a flare, hoping to save both drivers and doubters.

I do not speak because I enjoy confrontation; I speak because silence would be betrayal.

3. The Night We Forgot

We were not born ignorant; we were educated into amnesia. Generations learned to equate holiness with whiteness and humility with weakness.

The Great Forgetting (as I called it earlier in Volume 1) turned warriors into workers, prophets into performers. We traded covenant for culture. That night of forgetting still lingers in many minds.

But dawn is breaking. The Spirit is whispering through dreams, research, and revelation. People are waking up without preachers, just by reading the Word honestly. The Father is reclaiming His family one realization at a time.

✡

4. What I Have Seen

I have seen grandmothers cry when they discover that the Book they clutched all their lives was their family history. I have watched young men who once mocked Scripture weep as they realize they are descendants of the very prophets they dismissed.

I have seen marriages heal when both spouses understood that covenant love mirrors divine love. I have seen addicts find discipline through the law they once feared.

The awakening is not theory—it is testimony. Wherever truth is preached with patience, transformation follows.

5. My Own Repentance

Do not think I write from pedestal. I too had to repent—from pride, from anger, from despair. There was a time when I looked at the world and wanted vengeance, not victory. I wanted the oppressor punished more than the oppressed purified.

The Most High corrected me: "My justice needs no bitterness."

Now I teach from mercy. Every messenger must pass through humility or his message becomes hypocrisy. The covenant changes no one it cannot first correct.

6. Why Identity Still Matters

Some argue that heritage distracts from holiness. I say holiness without heritage becomes hollow.

When a people do not know who they are, they cannot know what obedience means. You cannot keep a covenant if you do not know you are in one.

Identity grounds behavior. When you know you are Hebrew, you treat yourself and others differently. You stop imitating nations that profit from your confusion. You realize you are not begging for a seat at the table—you are reclaiming the table your ancestors built.

7. To the Skeptics

I understand your doubts. The world has sold too many counterfeits to accept another claim easily.

So do not take my word alone—study for yourself. Read Deuteronomy 28, Jeremiah 17, Isaiah 11, and Revelation 7.

Research migration patterns, tribal customs, and linguistic roots. Compare prophecy with history. You will find the fingerprints of The Most High all over our story.

And when understanding comes, do not boast—bow. Knowledge without kneeling becomes arrogance.

8. To the Preachers

Some of you fear losing congregations if you preach this truth. I tell you: better lose members than lose your mandate.

The flock belongs to YAH, not to denominational boards. Preach identity with integrity. Do not replace grace with genealogy, but do not erase genealogy from grace. Teach balance—law and love, heritage and humility.

The gospel was never meant to erase Israel but to redeem her. Tell the people that salvation and self-knowledge are not rivals; they are relatives.

✡

9. To the Young and Restless

You feel it—the pull toward purpose. The world offers platforms without principles. It will pay you to mock righteousness, reward you for rebellion, and discard you once usefulness fades.

Choose covenant instead. The Most High is recruiting soldiers of light, innovators who code and create under holiness.

Do not let Babylon seduce you with speed. Move at the pace of prayer. Holiness may seem slow, but it always arrives on time. Build businesses that bless. Use art to awaken. You are not entertainers of the end times; you are architects of restoration.

✡

10. To the Elders

Your wisdom is the library of our liberation. Speak it while breath remains. Write your memories, record your testimonies.

The young cannot inherit what you hide. Many of you watched truth suppressed and stayed silent to survive; now speak to heal. The next generation needs your scars as maps.

Honor no longer comes from age alone but from accuracy. Teach the law, the lineage, the lessons of endurance. You are the bridge between forgetting and remembering.

11. The False Unity Trap

The world preaches unity without truth—"Let us all just get along," they say, while stepping on the backs of the righteous.

True unity begins with honesty. You cannot unite a people under lies.

The covenant does not demand segregation, but it forbids dilution.

We can love everyone while still knowing who we are. Salt loses savor when it blends too completely.

Unity built on deception crumbles; unity built on truth endures.

12. The Enemies of Restoration

Every restoration has its enemies: ignorance, fear, greed, and distraction.

- **Ignorance** says, "It doesn't matter."

- **Fear** says, "They'll hate us if we know."

- **Greed** says, "There's profit in confusion."

- **Distraction** says, "Maybe later."

Conquer all four daily. Study until ignorance flees. Pray until fear dissolves. Give until greed starves. Focus until distraction dies. The Most High equips those who persist.

13. The Danger of Idolatry in Awakening

Some awaken only to idolize their awakening. They trade one false image for another—worshiping lineage more than the Lord.

Beware that trap. Heritage is holy only when it leads to holiness. The goal is not to exalt the Hebrew but to exalt the Holy One of Israel.

If pride grows where repentance should, the awakening will dim. Keep your eyes on the Giver, not the gift.

✡

14. How to Continue the Work

1. **Study** daily—Scripture first, history second.

2. **Live clean**—diet, speech, habits.

3. **Build community**—support one another economically and spiritually.

4. **Teach children** truth before the world lies.

5. **Forgive freely**—bitterness is Babylon's perfume.

6. **Stay humble**—pride kills movement.

Do these things and the message will outlive every messenger.

15. My Prayer for the People

Father YAH, open our eyes where pride has blinded them. Heal the wounds our ancestors carried into our blood. Teach us to obey joyfully, to love justly, to speak wisely. Let our remembrance bring honor to Your name.

Gather the scattered, comfort the weary, correct the wandering. Let every Hebrew heart beat again with holiness. And let every nation see through us the reflection of Your mercy. Amen and Selah.

16. What Restoration Looks Like

Restoration is not shouting louder than others; it is shining brighter. It looks like fathers returning home, mothers resting from worry, children learning purpose early.

It looks like businesses that bless instead of exploit, neighborhoods without hunger, elders respected, youth employed, worship honest.

The world calls it reform; Heaven calls it repentance manifested. That is the proof of real awakening—not arguments won but lives rebuilt.

17. When You Feel Alone

Every prophet feels loneliness. When you tell truth that unsettles comfort, isolation becomes familiar. But solitude is sanctuary, not sentence.

The Most High trains His soldiers in silence. Use that quiet to strengthen prayer. Even Yeshua withdrew to mountains to recharge.

Do not mistake absence of applause for absence of approval. Heaven nods while earth glares.

18. Forgiveness for Our Fathers

We cannot heal while hating history. Some of our ancestors compromised, collaborated, or conformed. Forgive them. They survived the only way they knew. The same mercy that reached us will reach them. We break generational curses by releasing generational grudges. Forgiveness is inheritance; pass it on.

19. Vision for the Future

I see a future where "Black" is replaced by "Blessed," where children introduce themselves as Hebrews with humility, where cities once known for violence host festivals of worship, where agriculture replaces addiction, where faith replaces fear.

I see our people trading protest signs for plowshares, turning slogans into schools.

I see unity without uniformity, diversity without division.

That future is not fantasy—it is prophecy waiting for participation.

✡

20. To the Next Messengers

Someone reading this will take the baton. You will speak louder, travel farther, write deeper. Do not change the core: truth plus love. Avoid arrogance disguised as activism.

Let your scholarship be soaked in Spirit. Correct others gently; build more than you criticize. Remember, every messenger represents the message.

If they ignore you, keep speaking. Seeds do not complain when soil resists; they simply keep growing.

21. The Return of Honor

Honor will return when we live honorably. Men must treat women as partners, not possessions. Women must treat men as protectors, not predators.

Elders must guide, not gossip. Youth must listen, not mock. When we restore honor, the world will recognize holiness again. No revival can last where respect is dead.

Honor begins with how we speak, continues in how we serve, and ends in how we forgive.

22. Why We Must Keep Hope

The battle is long, and news headlines scream despair. But hope is the weapon darkness cannot counterfeit. Hope built our ancestors' songs and will build our children's future.

The Most High never abandons His covenant. Even when we wander, His promise follows. Every sunrise is proof that grace renewed overnight.

Hold hope like armor. Speak it, sing it, sow it. Hope is holy defiance.

23. Final Appeal to the Reader

If you have read this far, you are no longer innocent of ignorance. You know who you are. Now live it. Change vocabulary, habits, holidays, priorities.

Teach one other person what you learned here. Start small but start now. Heaven measures motion, not magnitude.

Do not wait for permission. You already have assignment. You are covenant people; act accordingly.

24. My Farewell and Faith

I may never meet you face-to-face, but if these words ignite remembrance, we are family.

The same bloodline that flowed through prophets flows through you. The same Spirit that hovered over creation hovers still. The same covenant written on tablets is now written on hearts.

Remember: The enemy fears a people who know both who they are and Whose they are.

Walk in that awareness daily. Let repentance be your rhythm, righteousness your reputation, restoration your reward.

I leave you with the charge Moses gave our ancestors:

"Choose life, that both thou and thy seed may live."

Choose it again today. Choose it tomorrow. Choose it until death itself gives up trying to stop you.

25. Closing Blessing

May YAH's face shine upon you and erase every false label. May His favor find you in famine and His peace surround your purpose. May your household know harmony, your mind clarity, your heart courage. May the nations see your light and call you blessed. And may you finish what our ancestors began: The return of the covenant people— healed, humble, and holy.

CHAPTER 11
Epilogue — The Eternal Witness

"And I will set My rainbow in the cloud, and it shall be for a sign of the covenant between Me and the earth." — Genesis 9 : 13

"Heaven and earth shall pass away, but My words shall not pass away." — Matthew 24 : 35

There are no endings in eternity—only echoes that fade into new songs. The awakening that began in whispers has become testimony written across generations. From the cries of bondage to the chants of liberation, from exile to enlightenment, the covenant people have walked the long road from forgetting to remembering. The journey itself has become scripture.

The world once tried to erase them with chains, wars, and lies, but truth is immune to extinction. It hides in language, in rhythm, in skin, in conscience. It waits patiently for the appointed season, then blossoms again through those willing to bear its fragrance. Every time a child of the diaspora calls on the Name, every time a heart turns from hate to holiness, the covenant renews itself.

History is a witness. Prophecy is a witness. And within each awakened soul, the Eternal Witness stirs—the same divine consciousness that watched creation's dawn and still whispers light into every breath.

The Hebrews scattered to every horizon are no longer fugitives of fate but gardeners of destiny. Their awakening redeems not only themselves but the memory of humanity. They are the living proof that no promise fails, that no people perish when they carry truth in their blood. The same law that sustained their ancestors now sustains their rebirth. The same mercy that followed them through deserts now waits at the gates of dawn.

The Eternal Witness does not sleep. He has recorded every tear shed in exile, every prayer uttered in chains, every act of kindness given in obscurity. Those tears are now ink; those prayers are now architecture; those acts are the blueprints of a world reborn. The new Jerusalem rises not from marble but from memory—each righteous remembrance another brick in its foundation.

When the world looks for proof of divinity, it will find it not in monuments of stone but in hearts that have endured fire and still choose forgiveness. The Hebrews are that living monument, their endurance the testimony, their faith the inscription: The Most High keeps covenant forever.

Volume I declared identity. Volume II built evidence. Volume III will reveal destiny—how the reborn covenant people lead all nations into equilibrium with the Creator's rhythm, how the scattered light becomes a single flame. For now, the work continues quietly in every home that honors truth, in every song that heals, in every conscience that refuses corruption.

The Eternal Witness watches, not as judge alone but as joy—rejoicing to see His children remember Him again. The covenant breathes through them, speaks through them, sings through them. Their story, long suppressed, has become the world's compass, pointing north toward righteousness.

The rainbow still arcs across heaven, unchanged since Noah's day. It bends not downward but around—encircling every tongue, tribe, and lineage that chooses light. Its message remains the same: the promise stands.

And beneath that promise, every generation adds its verse to the everlasting psalm. The melody began before the earth cooled, and it will continue long after galaxies forget their names. For truth does not die—it reincarnates as those who remember it.

The Eternal Witness smiles, and the world exhales. The covenant lives. The people live. The story continues.

✡

Personal Reflection & Quick Note to Reader

Beloved Reader:

if you have come this far, then you have walked through centuries in a matter of pages.

You have crossed deserts and oceans, endured exile and rebirth, stood at Sinai, and knelt in cotton fields — all without leaving your chair.

You have traced the path of a people who forgot their name yet never lost their God.

And now you stand where they stand: between what was taken and what must be reclaimed.

These writings were never intended merely to inform. They were written to transform — to awaken your remembrance and restore your reflection of the Most High.

Because truth, once learned, becomes a mirror: it shows you not only who your ancestors were but who you are expected to become.

1. The Purpose of Knowledge

Some study these things to prove others wrong. I studied and wrote them so that you might prove yourself right — not by argument but by action.

History is powerful, but holiness is greater.
Identity gives direction, but integrity gives destiny. It is not enough to know you are Hebrew; you must live as Hebrew — keeping faith, loving mercy, standing for justice, forgiving quickly, and walking humbly before your Creator.

The Most High has never required perfection, only obedience and progress. And every step toward righteousness strengthens not only you but generations unborn.

2. A Word to the Seekers of Every Faith

To the Christian who loves Christ, the Muslim who honors Allah, the Jew who upholds Torah, the Hindu who pursues dharma, the Buddhist who walks the Middle Way, and the skeptic who simply seeks truth: this book was written not to divide you but to remind you that righteousness has one origin — the Holy One who formed us all.

Each sincere faith carries a spark of His light, yet the Hebrew covenant remains the lampstand that first bore it. When we walk together in that light, darkness loses its dominion.

You need not convert to truth; you need only align with it.

Goodness is older than any religion and wider than any border.

3. The Call to the Descendants of the Covenant

To my brothers and sisters of the diaspora — those called Black, African-American, Afro-Caribbean, Afro-Latino, Hebrew, or Moor: you are the living evidence of prophecy fulfilled.

Your survival itself is Scripture come to life. Every field you worked, every prayer you whispered, every song you sang — all were chapters in the ongoing Book of Exodus.

The time of remembering has come. The dry bones breathe again. But memory alone is not enough.
The covenant must be kept.

Let your homes be sanctuaries, your families your first congregations, your labor your offering, and your life your sermon.

Rise each day determined to be a walking testimony that the Most High still reigns and still redeems.

4. From Knowledge to Nationhood

Identity without unity is noise. Unity without righteousness is rebellion. The awakening we are witnessing is not a fad; it is the foundation of a spiritual nation — one that transcends geography and politics. Its citizens are bound not by documents but by discipline, not by color but by covenant.

When we govern ourselves by divine law, we govern the world by example. And when we heal our own divisions, we become healers of the nations. This is the mission of the Hebrew reborn — not supremacy, but service.

5. The Promise Ahead

Prophecy has already begun to unfold: the scattered are remembering; the proud are humbling; the righteous are rising. But the greatest fulfillment is yet to come.

When you forgive those who wronged you, you disarm captivity. When you build instead of beg, you reverse the curse. When you teach your children who they are and Whose they are, you restore Zion one household at a time.

Never forget — your history did not begin in slavery, and your destiny does not end in struggle. You are not cursed; you are called. Not forsaken; but foretold. Not lost; but found.

6. A Final Benediction

May the Most High Yah bless your mind with clarity, your heart with courage, your hands with purpose, and your home with peace.

May your name be restored, your lineage remembered, and your light never dim.

May you walk in such obedience that your children inherit freedom not just in law but in spirit. And may the nations see through you the faithfulness of the God of Abraham, Isaac, and Jacob.

Let every reader become the evidence that truth still lives — that prophecy still breathes — that the covenant still stands.

"For ye are the children of light and the children of the day." — 1 Thessalonians 5 : 5

"Arise, shine; for thy light is come, and the glory of the LORD is risen upon thee." — Isaiah 60 : 1

Now go live as proof. Not Black. Not African-American. You are Hebrew.

APPENDIX A
Concordance of Parallels: The Voice of Truth in All Scriptures

"For precept must be upon precept, line upon line."
— Isaiah 28 : 10

"The truth is one; sages call it by many names." — Rig Veda 1 .164 .46

The Creator Is One

From the beginning, revelation has testified to oneness.

The Torah declares, "Hear, O Israel: The LORD our God, the LORD is One." (Deuteronomy 6 : 4).

Centuries later, Paul reaffirmed it in the Bible, writing, "There is none other God but one." (1 Corinthians 8 : 4).

The Qur'an proclaims with absolute simplicity, "Say: He is Allah, the One and Only." (Surah Al-Ikhlas 112 : 1).

Even outside the Abrahamic line, Buddhist and Hindu sages echoed the same truth: "The wise understand that the Truth is one, though paths differ," (Udana 8 : 3) and "There is one Supreme Being who pervades all." (Bhagavad Gita 13 : 27).

Thus, whether spoken in Hebrew, Greek, Arabic, Pali, or Sanskrit, humanity has always known there is one Source of all life.

✡

The Chosen and the Covenant

The Torah announces, "For thou art a holy people unto the LORD thy God... He has chosen thee to be a special people unto Himself." (Deuteronomy 7 : 6).

The New Testament mirrors this calling: "You are a chosen generation, a royal priesthood." (1 Peter 2 : 9).

The Qur'an reminds the world, "O Children of Israel, remember My favor which I bestowed upon you, and that I preferred you above the nations." (Surah Al-Baqarah 2 : 47).

Even the Dhammapada teaches, "Few are those who walk the path; they are the light of the world." and the Bhagavad Gita records God saying, "Whenever righteousness declines, I manifest Myself to restore dharma." (4 : 7).

Across continents, Heaven chooses vessels of light to keep moral order alive; among them, the Hebrews stand as the original witnesses of covenant responsibility.

✡

Justice and Righteousness

Every sacred record exalts justice as the evidence of true faith.

The Torah commands, "Justice, justice shalt thou pursue." (Deuteronomy 16 : 20).

The prophet Micah echoes, "Do justice, love mercy, and walk humbly with thy God." (Micah 6 : 8).

The Qur'an elevates justice above kinship: "Stand firmly for justice, as witnesses for Allah, even against yourselves." (An-Nisa 4 : 135).

Buddha taught, "Conquer anger by love, evil by good, the miser by giving, and the liar by truth." and the Gita counsels, "Perform your duty with righteousness, for action is greater than inaction." (3 : 8).

The divine law has never changed—wherever righteousness rules, oppression fades.

Compassion and Forgiveness

Holiness is incomplete without mercy.

The Torah commands, "Love your neighbor as yourself." (Leviticus 19 : 18).

Yeshua confirmed, "Forgive, and you will be forgiven." (Luke 6 : 37).

The Qur'an honors the humble: "The servants of the Most Merciful walk humbly on the earth... and when the ignorant address them, they say, 'Peace.'" (Al-Furqan 25 : 63).

The Buddha revealed, "Hatred does not cease by hatred; by love alone it ceases."

And Krishna describes the righteous soul: "He who is free from malice toward all beings, friendly and compassionate, humble and patient, that man is dear to Me." (12 : 13).

All agree—compassion is the crown of divine likeness.

Discipline and Obedience

True liberty flows from obedience to divine law.

Moses wrote, "Keep His statutes and commandments that it may go well with thee." (Deuteronomy 4 : 40).

Yeshua said, "Blessed are they that hear the word of God and keep it." (Luke 11 : 28).

The Qur'an affirms, "The most honored of you in the sight of Allah is the most righteous of you." (Al-Hujurat 49 : 13).

Buddha taught, "Better than a thousand hollow words is one word that brings peace."

The Gita calls such self-control "divine wealth— control of mind and senses, purity of heart, steadfastness in truth." (16 : 1-3).

Discipline turns belief into power; it is how the covenant lives inside conduct.

The Promise of Restoration

The Torah comforts Israel: "When you return to the LORD your God... He will turn your captivity and have compassion upon you." (Deuteronomy 30 : 2-3).

Yeshua foretold the gathering: "He will send His angels to gather His elect from the four winds." (Matthew 24 : 31).

The Qur'an remembers this same promise: "We said to the Children of Israel: 'Dwell in the land; and when the promise of the Hereafter comes, We shall bring you forth as a mixed assembly.'" (Al-Isra 17 : 104).

Buddha spoke likewise of return: "Those who walk in righteousness return again to the seat of peace." and the Gita echoes, "The soul returns to the eternal dwelling, freed from the cycles of ignorance." (8 : 15).

Every tradition looks toward restoration; the Hebrew awakening fulfills them all.

The Light and the Law

Scripture describes divine wisdom as illumination.

"For the commandment is a lamp, and the law is light." (Proverbs 6 : 23).

Yeshua expanded, "You are the light of the world." (Matthew 5 : 14).

The Qur'an declares, "Allah is the Light of the heavens and the earth." (An-Nur 24 : 35).

The Buddha urged, "Be a lamp unto yourselves; hold fast to truth as your light."

And the Gita identifies the same eternal radiance: "The light of all lights, dwelling beyond darkness, is the Supreme." (13 : 17).

Light, in every faith, represents law in motion.

The Unity of Humanity

Though Israel is chosen, creation is one family.

Malachi asks, "Have we not all one Father? Hath not one God created us?" (Malachi 2 : 10).

Paul writes, "God has made of one blood all nations of men." (Acts 17 : 26).

The Qur'an echoes: "We created you male and female and made you nations and tribes that you may know one another." (Al-Hujurat 49 : 13).

Buddha taught the Metta Sutta: "As a mother watches over her child, so with boundless heart should one cherish all living beings."

And the Upanishads reveal, "He who sees all beings in the Self and the Self in all beings — he sees truly." (Isha Upanishad 6).

The covenant people honor God best by honoring His creation.

The Reward for Good Works

Moses wrote, "If you walk in My statutes... I will give you rain in due season and peace in your land." (Leviticus 26 : 3-6).

Paul encouraged, "Be not weary in well-doing; in due season we shall reap if we faint not." (Galatians 6 : 9).

The Qur'an assures, "Whoever does good, male or female, while a believer—We will surely cause him to live a good life." (An-Nahl 16 : 97).

Buddha declared, "From good arises good; from evil arises evil. Whoever acts with pure mind, happiness follows as a shadow."

The Gita teaches, "Every action, good or bad, brings its result; only right intention purifies the act." (4 : 20).

Heaven's economy never fails—the harvest matches the seed.

The End of Oppression and the Coming Kingdom

Prophecy across scriptures foresees an age of peace. Isaiah promised, "Nation shall not lift up sword against nation, neither shall they learn war any more." (2 : 4).

Revelation repeats, "The kingdoms of this world are become the kingdoms of our Lord and of His Christ." (11 : 15).

The Qur'an envisions, "The earth will shine with the light of its Lord, and justice shall be established." (Az-Zumar 39 : 69).

Buddha said, "Peace comes not through conquest but through understanding."

The Bhagavata Purana foretells, "When righteousness is established and evil subdued, the age of truth shall return."

Every creed looks toward a single destiny—the reign of divine justice on earth.

Closing Reflection

Truth is a river that began in Eden, flowed through Sinai, crossed into Zion, Medina, Lumbini, and the Ganges. Its waters reach every land, yet the source remains one. The covenant given to Abraham, Isaac, and Jacob did not expire — it expanded.

And as the scattered descendants of those ancient Hebrews awaken in this generation, they are called to recognize that fragments of their light survive in every faith tradition. We study these parallels not to imitate other paths but to see how the Hebrew current of righteousness irrigated the whole earth.

"For the earth shall be filled with the knowledge of the glory of the LORD, as the waters cover the sea." — Habakkuk 2 : 14

The same God who spoke to Moses on Sinai, to Yeshua in Galilee, to Muhammad in the cave, to the rishis beneath the banyan tree, and to the Buddha beneath the bodhi tree still speaks now—to you.

Listen, remember, and walk in truth.

APPENDIX B
Historical Timeline Of The Scattered Tribes

"Thou shalt be removed into all the kingdoms of the earth." — Deuteronomy 28 : 25

"They shall remember themselves in the land of their captivity." — Baruch 2 : 30

✡

1 · The Ancient Covenant People (-2000 to -600 BCE)

The story begins with Abraham, a Hebrew nomad from Ur, who entered a covenant with the Most High around two millennia BCE. His descendants — Isaac, Jacob, and the twelve tribes of Israel — became a distinct people charged to guard divine law. Under Moses (circa -1400 BCE), they were delivered from Egypt and given the Torah at Sinai, forming the first nation built entirely upon covenant ethics rather than political conquest.

From Joshua through David and Solomon, Israel rose to prominence. Jerusalem's temple became the moral center of the known world. But prosperity brought pride; idolatry entered the land. Prophets like Isaiah, Jeremiah, and Amos warned that disobedience would end in exile — prophecies that later generations would literally fulfill.

2 · The Exiles and Dispersions (-722 to -586 BCE)

The northern Kingdom of Israel fell first, conquered by Assyria in -722 BCE. The ten tribes were taken away and scattered across Asia and Africa, some migrating south through Egypt and Kush. A century later, Babylon captured Judah and destroyed Solomon's temple (-586 BCE). The prophets wept; the people walked in chains. Yet even in captivity they preserved the Sabbath, the dietary laws, and the songs of Zion — the spiritual DNA that no empire could erase.

3 · Return, Occupation, and Diaspora (-538 BCE to 70 CE)

When Persia conquered Babylon, Cyrus the Great permitted the Hebrews to return and rebuild. Many did, yet many remained abroad, forming communities throughout Mesopotamia, Arabia, Ethiopia, and Egypt. By the time of Yeshua Ha-Mashiach, Israelites lived on three continents. After Rome's destruction of the Second Temple in 70 CE, the final dispersion began. Hebrew refugees fled into North Africa, Arabia, Spain, and the Western Sudan — regions that would later seed the trans-Saharan and trans-Atlantic worlds.

4 · The African Hebrew Presence (1st – 15th centuries CE)

Centuries before Europe's rise, Hebrew culture flourished across Africa. In Ethiopia, the Beta Israel maintained Mosaic traditions; in Sudan and Chad, remnants of the Levitical order taught laws of purity and sacrifice. Hebrew traders settled among the Yoruba, Igbo, Akan, Mali, and Songhai, interweaving Torah customs with local life. Oral histories, clan names such as Abia, Levi, and Ben-Eri, and linguistic roots trace directly to Semitic speech.

The Moorish empires of North Africa also carried this memory, blending Hebrew, Berber, and Arab ancestry. The Bey and El titles that appear centuries later among African-descended people in America descend from these communities of covenant-keepers who survived Rome and Islam alike.

5 · The Rise of Empires and Enslavement (15th – 19th centuries CE)

When Portugal and Spain began exploring West Africa, they encountered advanced kingdoms — Benin, Ghana, Mali — where elements of Hebrew law persisted.

These encounters triggered Europe's appetite for gold, ivory, and eventually captives. As the Atlantic slave trade expanded, millions of West and Central Africans — many from tribes maintaining Sabbath, circumcision, and covenant taboos — were shipped across the ocean.

They were not mere slaves; they were the physical continuation of Israel's scattered seed. The ships of Deuteronomy 28 : 68 sailed again. Their languages carried traces of Hebrew consonants; their songs carried psalms. Even chained, they prayed to the God of Abraham. In the Americas, that memory evolved into spirituals, ring-shouts, and call-and-response worship that paralleled ancient temple liturgy.

6 · Captivity in the New World (1600s – 1800s)

In the plantations of the Americas, the prophecy of oppression replayed with exact precision. Families were divided; names changed; Sabbath replaced by labor. Yet within the darkness, revelation whispered. The enslaved Hebrews saw their story in Moses and Pharaoh, in Egypt and Exodus. "Go Down Moses" was more than a song — it was encoded Scripture.

By the 19th century, abolitionists of African descent began publishing biblical arguments linking their suffering to Israel's exile. Preachers such as Nat Turner, Frederick

Douglass, and Maria Stewart used the Mosaic narrative as proof that God would free His covenant people again.

✡

7 · Revelation and Reclamation (1800s – 1900s)

After emancipation, newly freed Africans in the Americas sought meaning for their survival. Many turned instinctively toward Old Testament law, forming congregations that kept feast days, dietary rules, and Hebrew names. In the early 20th century, movements such as the Commandment Keepers in Harlem and the Church of God and Saints of Christ proclaimed that African-Americans were descendants of Israel.

Simultaneously, the Moorish Science Temple, led by Prophet Noble Drew Ali, taught national and spiritual identity rooted in Afro-Asiatic heritage. Titles like Bey and El resurfaced as public affirmations of nobility and faith. These parallel awakenings, though differing in form, all served one prophecy: that the lost tribes would remember themselves.

✡

8 · Modern Awakening (20th – 21st centuries)

In the mid-1900s, Hebrew identity movements multiplied. Scholars documented Semitic customs among the

Igbo of Nigeria and the Lemba of southern Africa, whose priestly DNA markers traced to the Levites of Israel. In America, teachers blended biblical exegesis with linguistic and anthropological proof.

By the 1970s and '80s, groups calling themselves Hebrew Israelites, African Hebrews, and Kingdom Cultural Assemblies expanded nationwide. Some migrated to Israel itself, establishing the Village of Peace in Dimona. Others built communities in Chicago, New York, Atlanta, and Jackson, Mississippi, linking heritage to civic empowerment.

The internet age removed the final veil. DNA research, digitized archives, and global communication reconnected descendants across oceans. Youth who once knew only labels like Black or African-American began studying Torah, Hebrew language, and ancestry. Prophecy and technology met.

✡

9 · The Present Hour

Today, awakening accelerates. Elders, pastors, imams, and scholars now revisit old assumptions; interfaith dialogues reveal the same ancestral thread running through African and Middle-Eastern bloodlines. Historians uncover suppressed records showing early Jewish and Hebrew communities throughout West Africa long before colonial contact.

The call is no longer limited to race or geography. The awakening invites every descendant of the scattered tribes — and every soul seeking truth — to live by covenant principles: honesty, justice, chastity, mercy, and reverence for the Creator. The physical return to Zion begins first as a spiritual return to obedience.

10 · Prophetic Fulfillment and The Future

Scripture promises that the scattered will gather again. "He will lift up a banner for the nations and assemble the outcasts of Israel." (Isaiah 11 : 12).

The modern rise of identity, education, and unity among African-descended peoples marks the early stages of that fulfillment. The dry bones of Ezekiel's vision now breathe.

Whether in America, Africa, or the Caribbean, the descendants of the covenant are rebuilding. Music, art, and moral reform signal that the Spirit of Yah is restoring His people's dignity. Yet this revival demands humility: the world will not be healed by pride but by righteousness. The purpose of rediscovered identity is service — to guide humanity back toward law, light, and love.

Closing Reflection

From Abraham's tents to American plantations, from the Red Sea to the Mississippi, the story has been one continuous pilgrimage of a chosen people who lost their names but not their God. Empires have risen and fallen, yet the covenant remains.

Now the descendants stand at a crossroads. History has proven their lineage; prophecy calls them to live worthy of it. The final chapter of exile is being written not by governments but by individual hearts that choose truth over titles.

When righteousness again defines our culture, language, and labor, Zion will no longer be a dream but a reality reborn.

"And I will plant them upon their land, and they shall no more be pulled up." — Amos 9 : 15

APPENDIX C
Glossary of Hebrew & Afro-Asiatic Names

"For then will I turn to the peoples a pure language, that they may all call upon the name of the LORD, to serve Him with one consent." — Zephaniah 3 : 9

1 · The Sacred Foundations

Long before slavery or colonization, names among the covenant people carried spiritual assignments. Each word bore witness to God's nature, covenant, or promise. Even after foreign tongues reshaped pronunciation, the meanings endured. What follows are some of the principal Hebrew and Afro-Asiatic roots still echoed in modern African and diasporic names.

Ab / Aba / Oba — "Father / King"

From the Hebrew Ab ("father") appears African parallels such as Oba among the Yoruba ("king") and Aba in Ghana ("born on Thursday"). These variants testify that patriarchal and royal titles shared one sacred origin: the recognition of divine fatherhood and authority.

El / Eli / Eliyahu — "My God / The Most High is Yah"

El means "God" in Hebrew and appears throughout Scripture: El Shaddai, El Elyon. Names ending in -el—like Michael ("Who is like God?") or Daniel ("God is my Judge")—were preserved across continents. The suffix -elu or -eluwa found in Igbo and Congo names (Chukwuelu, Eluwa) mirrors that same reverent form.

Yah / Yahu / Yahuah — "The Self-Existent One"

Root of the divine name revealed to Moses: YHWH. African tongues retained its rhythm: Yaa, Yahu, Yaya. Diasporic believers revived it as "Yah," proclaiming Hallelu-Yah—"Praise Yah." In many African spiritual songs, even under Christian or Muslim overlay, this syllable remained untouched.

Ben / Beni / Obinna — "Son / Descendant / Child of Grace"

Hebrew Ben ("son of") reappears in countless African clan names—Ben-Ali, Beni-Yah, Bene Israel. In Nigeria, Obinna literally means "father's heart," identical in sentiment to the Hebrew concept of filial blessing.

Levi / Lewi / Lewe — "Joined / Attached"

From the priestly tribe of Levi. Across Africa, Lewi and Lewe denote priestly or clan leadership roles. Even among early African-American surnames, "Levy" survived as both occupation and remembrance of priesthood.

Melek / Malik / Molok — "King / Ruler"

Hebrew Melek means "king"; Arabic Malik carries the same. Among the Moors and later African-Americans, Malik and Melek signified nobility and divine stewardship—echoes of the Davidic throne.

Bey / Beg / Baai — "Chief / Governor / Noble Son"

Derived from ancient Afro-Asiatic and Turkic honorifics meaning "lord" or "leader." Adopted by Moors and African Hebrews during the Islamic and Ottoman periods, Bey became a badge of restored dignity. In the Americas, it symbolized reclaiming lawful identity after centuries of denigration—"Bey" marking the bearer as a person of covenant rank.

El / Bey / Ali — Twin Pillars of Restoration

In Moorish-Hebrew tradition, El represents spiritual divinity and Bey civic sovereignty. Ali, from Arabic ʿAliyy ("elevated"), often joined them to create compound names like Ali Bey El. Together they proclaim: "I am noble by God's decree, not man's permission."

2 · Tribal and Regional Continuities

Yoruba

Names such as Oluwaseun ("Thank God"), Obadare ("King of Wonder"), and Oluwatoyin ("God is worthy to be praised") reflect unmistakable Hebraic grammar—prefixes meaning God followed by verbs of praise.

Igbo

The Igbo of Nigeria preserve entire genealogies aligned with Israelite custom: male circumcision on the eighth day, separation laws, and festival offerings. Names like Chukwuemeka ("God has done greatly") and Ezekwe ("God says") retain Hebrew syntax.

Akan / Ashanti / Ewe

Tribal names such as Kwame, Afua, Kojo were originally calendar-based like ancient Hebrew reckonings of sacred days. The term Ewe itself, pronounced Eh-veh, parallels Eber—ancestor of the Hebrews (Genesis 10 : 21).

Amharic / Ethiopian Hebrew

Words like Haile ("power"), Selassie ("trinity / threefold power"), and Tafari ("he who inspires awe") preserve Semitic structure. The Ethiopian Beta Israel community still uses original Hebrew prayers.

3 · Names Born in Captivity and Reclaimed in Freedom

During enslavement, surnames were stripped away; biblical names were all that remained. Yet these adopted names became codes of remembrance. Isaiah, Ezra, Mary, Moses, Joshua—names whispered on plantations as prophecy that deliverance would come again.

In the 20th century, reclamation intensified. African-American families revived ancient titles: Bey, El, Ali, Yisrael, Ben Yah, Yahudah. Each addition was more than style; it was identity reborn. A people once cataloged as property began renaming themselves as promise.

4 · Sacred Meanings Restored

To the awakened Hebrew, a name is never cosmetic. It is covenant compressed into sound. When a person bears a divine root—Yah, El, Ben, Malak, Shalom—they proclaim daily what history tried to silence: that they belong to the Most High.

Even those who do not know Hebrew instinctively preserve its rhythm in gospel music, spoken word, and African dialects that still breathe the vowels of Eden.

Thus the rediscovery of true names is not vanity; it is healing. As Isaiah 44 : 5 foretold, "One shall say, 'I am the LORD's'; another shall call himself by the name of Jacob; and another shall subscribe with his hand unto the LORD, and surname himself by the name of Israel.'"

5 · Closing Reflection

Across ages and oceans, the children of the covenant have answered to many names—Hebrew, Moor, African, Negro, Colored, Black, and now Hebrew again.

Yet beneath every label beats the same heartbeat of divine lineage. When you speak your true name with understanding, you awaken ancestral memory and spiritual authority. Names are prayers; every syllable either binds or frees.

The journey from slave names to sacred names mirrors the greater journey from bondage to blessing. To know what your name means is to remember what you were made for: to represent the Creator with integrity, excellence, and love.

"They shall call on My name, and I will hear them. I will say, 'It is My people'; and they shall say, 'The LORD is my God.'" — Zechariah 13 : 9

ACKNOWLEDGMENTS

All praises and honor to The Most High Yah, the Eternal Source of wisdom, patience, and truth. Without His guidance, no revelation would have matured into writing, and no word of this book could have found its purpose.

I give humble thanks to every elder, scholar, and truth-seeker whose research and resilience kept the flame of Hebrew identity alive through centuries of suppression. To the early teachers of Moorish, Hebrew, and Pan-African heritage whose courage to question paved roads for those who came after—your labor was not in vain.

Deep respect to Bro. Jeffery Ellison, who honored his late brother Brother David Ellison-Bey by preserving his writings and extending the lineage of enlightenment. His foreword bridges generations and reminds us that truth transcends biology—it is the bloodline of spirit.

Gratitude to the readers of the first volume of **NOT BLACK. NOT AFRICAN-AMERICAN. YOU ARE HEBREW!** whose feedback, testimonies, and shared stories made this continuation necessary. Every conversation, every letter, every message reaffirmed that we are not lost—we are rediscovering ourselves together.

To the global family—those who call upon Yah, Allah, Krishna, Buddha, or simply the God within—thank you for proving that righteousness is a universal language.

May these pages strengthen unity, not competition; restoration, not rivalry.

To Dr. Mary Jefferson, Mylia Tiye Mal Jaza and crew, at BePublished.org — your capacity for optimal output in superhuman speed is just proof of The Most High's presence in your life and workings through you. You are an amazing woman of Yah and a true divine soul. I've never met anyone like you, but the world needs more people like you. Thank you for all you've done to help me do in one month what I wasn't able to do in 15 years before meeting you. May you be blessed to accomplish every goal you have for yourself and your family with the same speed and ease that you afford your clients.

Finally, to every person who stood beside me through late nights, deep study, and long prayer—you know who you are. May the blessings of the Most High multiply in your homes, your health, and your hearts.

THE ART & ARTIST

Volume II: *NOT BLACK. NOT AFRICAN-AMERICAN. YOU ARE HEBREW! — The Hidden Heritage & The Global Proof*

After awakening comes confirmation.

In the powerful second installment of Khalil Bey's historic trilogy, *The Hidden Heritage & The Global Proof* bridges prophecy with proof — combining scriptural insight, genetics, geography, and world history to validate the truth of the Hebrew identity hidden within the African diaspora.

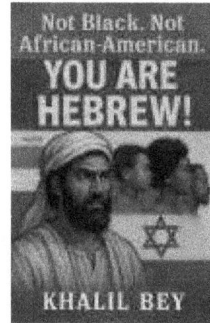

This volume goes beyond belief into evidence. Bey dismantles misconceptions with facts drawn from scripture, ancient maps, linguistic patterns, and archaeological findings, revealing how colonization and religion conspired to bury divine heritage under centuries of deception.

Here, history meets prophecy — and science agrees.

Written in the same compelling, accessible style as Volume I, this book shows readers that reclaiming Hebrew identity is not rebellion — it's restoration. And it isn't limited to one race, but rooted in one covenant.

"Faith stands strongest when it walks beside evidence." — Khalil Bey

Published in November 2025 alongside Volumes I and III plus a healing journal with assistance from BePublished.org, this second release serves as the cornerstone for truth-seekers who desire both faith and fact.

Open it — and rediscover the proof of who you are.

Available as a Kindle eBook globally, you may also purchase. ***Not Black. Not African-American. You Are Hebrew!*** by Khalil Bey as a printed paperback from online and bricks-and-mortar book resellers including your favorite bookstore. Order your copy today, or go ahead and get all three now.

THE AUTHOR

Khalil Bey is a messenger of truth, a student of scripture, and a witness of the awakening. Known for his bold yet balanced approach to spiritual identity and heritage, Khalil has dedicated his life to helping people remember who they are — and who they belong to.

Born in Chicago with a deep hunger for wisdom and understanding, Khalil spent years studying the Holy Scriptures, ancient history, and spiritual science across multiple traditions — including the Torah, Bible, Qur'an, Vedas, and Sutras.

His passion has always been to unite truth with evidence, faith with history, and revelation with reality. Before the world knew him as an author, Khalil was a student, a seeker, and a teacher within his community. He spoke in living rooms, on street corners, and online platforms — not for fame, but for faith. Through every challenge, he held to one conviction: that the Most High never forgets His covenant, and that His people must never forget their divine purpose.

After ten years of struggle to publish his work, Khalil's persistence paid off when his first book — *Not Black. Not African-American. You Are Hebrew!* — was released through **BePublished.org**, under the guidance of **Dr. Mary M. Jefferson**. That collaboration ignited a mission that would become a movement.

From the moment his first book was released, readers around the world began awakening to the truth of their divine heritage. The outpouring of response inspired Khalil to expand his vision into a full trilogy — each volume serving as a new layer of enlightenment:

- **Volume I – The Awakening:** A call to identity and spiritual rediscovery.

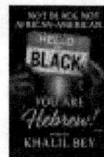

- **Volume II – The Hidden Heritage and the Global Proof:** A documentation of prophecy and history confirming the truth.

- **Volume III – The Age of Wisdom and the Universal Covenant:** A revelation of purpose, balance, and unity under divine law.

Together, these works form one complete message — a blueprint for living as a covenant people in a confused world.

And since the final portion of the third book was so large, Khalil decided to follow his publisher's advice and release a journal has his fourth work and stand-alone piece that serves as a companion to the trilogy to help heal wounds and best facilitate a continuance of this difficult walk we all have with The Most High.

Khalil's mission is simple but sacred: to teach truth, build faith, and restore dignity to those who were told they had none. He continues to write, teach, and serve as a voice for the Hebrew people — while welcoming all nations to walk in wisdom and light.

His prayer is that every reader, regardless of background, will discover their place in the

Most High's plan and live it boldly, righteously, and with love.

When asked what drives him, Khalil answers: "The truth doesn't need to be invented — it needs to be remembered. My job is just to remind the people of what was already written inside them."

He lives by faith, teaches by conviction, and serves by calling. And through every book, conversation, and connection, Khalil Bey continues to remind the world that: **Heritage is holy. Truth is timeless. And light always finds its way home.**